LESSONS FOR LIFE

Career Development Activities Library

Volume 1: Elementary Grades

Zark VanZandt

Bette Ann Buchan

Illustrations by Eileen Ciavarella

The Center for Applied
Research in Education
West Nyack, NY 10994

Library of Congress Cataloging-in-Publication Data

VanZandt, Zark.
    Lessons for life : career development / Zark VanZandt, Bettie Ann Buchan.
      p. cm.
    Includes bibliographical references.
    Contents: v. 1. Elementary level
    ISBN 0-87628-514-0
    1. Student aspirations. 2. Educational counseling. 3.Vocational guidance. 4. Career
education. 5.Life skills. I. VanZandt, Zark. II. Title.
LB10278.B83 1997
372.14'2--dc21   97-28088
                                                 CIP

Printed in the United States of America

10 9 8 7 6 5 4 3 2 1

ISBN 0-87628-514-0 (Spiral)

ATTENTION: CORPORATIONS AND SCHOOLS

The Center for Applied Research in Education books are available at quantity discounts with bulk purchase for educational, business, or sales promotional use. For information, please write to: Prentice Hall Career & Personal Development Special Sales, 240 Frisch Court, Paramus, NJ 07652. Please supply: title of book, ISBN number, quantity, how the book will be used, date needed.

**THE CENTER FOR APPLIED RESEARCH
IN EDUCATION**
West Nyack, NY 10994
A Simon & Schuster Company

On the World Wide Webb at http://www.phdirect.com

Prentice-Hall International (UK) Limited, *London*
Prentice-Hall of Australia Pty. Limited, *Sydney*
Prentice-Hall Canada, Inc., *Toronto*
Prentice-Hall Hispanoamericana, S.A., *Mexico*
Prentice-Hall of India Private Limited, *New Delhi*
Prentice-Hall of Japan, Inc., *Tokyo*
Simon & Schuster Asia Pte. Ltd., *Singapore*
Editora Prentice-Hall do Brasil, Ltda., *Rio de Janeiro*

About the Authors

Zark VanZandt is a counselor educator at the University of Southern Maine in Gorham. In the earlier part of his career journey, he was both an elementary and a high school counselor, a Director of Guidance, a state guidance consultant, and a counselor educator in two other states. Zark has presented workshops at the national, regional, and state levels, and has written articles for several journals and newsletters. Zark and Bette Ann previously collaborated on a Public Relations kit for the American School Counselor Association. His most recent professional activities have included his role as the project consultant for ASCA's *Get a Life* portfolio and as the coauthor of a textbook on comprehensive developmental school counseling programs. Zark received his B.A. and M.A. degrees from Michigan State University and his doctorate from the University of Maine. He resides in Gorham with his wife and three sons.

Bette Ann Buchan is an elementary/middle school counselor at Woolwich Central School, Woolwich, Maine, where she initiated and now implements a comprehensive K-8 guidance program. She came to that position with teaching experience ranging from kindergarten to adult. Outside the school setting, she consults for UNUM America in their Career Development and Resource Center and is an adjunct clinical supervisor for interns at the University of Southern Maine Counselor Education program. Bette Ann has presented workshops at the state, regional, and local levels on topics ranging from integrating music into classroom guidance lessons to public relations. She received her B.A. degree from St. Joseph's College in North Windham, Maine, and her M.Ed. in guidance and counseling from University of Central Oklahoma in Edmond. She resides in the town of Woolwich with her husband and two college-age children.

How to Use *Lessons for Life*

The activities in *Lessons for Life* were written by and for busy educators; written for teachers and counselors who want to lay their hands on a self-contained resource that has clear skill-based objectives, accessible supplies and available worksheets, a high-interest age-appropriate lesson design, and measurable outcomes. Those criteria were foundational to the creation of the lessons in this book.

Chapters 4 through 7 are organized according to the same categories used in the American School Counselor Association's *Get a Life* portfolio. As we mention elsewhere in the book, you do not have to be using the *Get a Life* portfolio to use and benefit from the lessons in this book. The four categories of Self-Knowledge, Life Roles, Educational Development, and Career Exploration and Planning are foundational components of almost any "good" career guidance program.

Each of the four chapters devoted to lesson plans has been divided into five subheadings, each containing three lessons. You now have 60 lessons (120 in the two-volume set) to aid students in the reflective process of examining who they are, how their life roles have developed, the relevance of their education, and the significant factors that contribute to positive career choices.

Most lessons can be completed in one 40-minute session. However, some "continued" lessons need additional time for such things as independent student research, written assignments, and interviews. Many lessons also have suggested follow-up activities; thus, facilitators are encouraged to extend the lessons with the suggested ideas or your own original ideas that might capitalize on the students' processing statements during the lesson's closure.

Reproducible worksheets have been developed for certain lessons. Other supplies commonly found in schools may also be needed (e.g., chart paper, markers) or may be readily available from students' homes. Some lessons may require resource materials found in the library or guidance and counseling office.

Each complete lesson is organized on two facing pages. The left sheet we refer to as the "Preview Page," where we list the lesson title, the career topic being addressed, the skill-based objectives, supplies needed, and an indication of where students' reflections about the lesson might be entered if you are using the *Get a Life* portfolio. It is suggested that the person facilitating the lesson spend at least a little time reviewing the objectives and organizing the supplies. Particular classes, because of students' unique learning needs or the significance of the topic, may require special accommodations, and a quick preview will help the facilitator be attentive to those needs.

The objectives of the lessons are skill-based, indicating what the students will know or be able to do after the lesson is completed. Two simple evaluation/feedback sheets are provided in the Epilogue section of this book to assist you in determining whether the objectives have been met. It may not be necessary to use such an assessment for every lesson, but the results of simple formative evaluations such as these can be helpful for suggesting changes or highlighting major successes. They can also be used as simple tools for promoting accountability in the delivery of the career development curriculum.

On the facing page is the actual lesson, including the Introduction, Focus, Activity, Closure, and sometimes a suggestion for a Follow-up Activity. A "Notes" section is also provided on this page so the person facilitating the lesson may make personal comments for additions or deletions to the lesson. This space for notes is a good place to make accommodations in the lessons and to record the insights and ideas that are a result of your own reflective practice. In the future, being prepared for changes in the lesson will contribute to the ease with which the instructor delivers the lesson and the students grasp the significance of the lesson.

The special ingredient that makes any lesson better is the enthusiasm of the facilitator, and it is often the critical factor in the lesson's success. With the continued use of the resources in *Lessons for Life,* and with the refinements you make in the "Notes" section of the lessons, you should be able to infuse your own enthusiasm in their delivery by noting the way the lessons complement your own career development journey, your personality and style, and the goals you have set for the curriculum's success. Because we are role models for young people as they make meaning of their lives and begin their own journeys and searches for careers that matter, our enthusiasm for that process will make a significant statement about how we value our students as individuals. Enjoy the journey.

Zark VanZandt
Bette Ann Buchan

"Life's Journey" as Metaphor

As we have reflected on the essence of this practical collection of resources for busy educators, we have felt a need to reiterate two important themes that have guided our efforts and defined our mission. The first theme is that of "career as life"; the second depicts career as a life journey.

All too often, *career* is seen as one's occupation or sequence of jobs. The perspective we want to promote—and it is reinforced by many Career Development scholars—is that one's career is an integration of several very important life roles. Our choices about how we balance the roles of family member, leisurite, citizen, spiritual being, friend, *and* worker will define the measure of our career success. Individuals must seek their own balance that fits their unique circumstances, and in creating that balance, their lives become more fulfilling. This is a lesson that needs to be taught early and often in the schools.

Obviously, the roles stated above will not remain stagnant, but will change according to an individual's circumstances, age, and personal life histories. For example, the role of family member may be more prominent when a child is dependent on a parent—or vice versa. At other times in a person's life, a spiritual component may take on greater emphasis and meaning, for a variety of reasons. Students in graduate school often lament the absence of leisure activities in their lives. As schools help students understand these interdependent roles, they can be instrumental in providing the knowledge and skills to cope with life's passages and changes. If one's career is seen as one's life, not one's job, then the individual can begin to see that life is a process of understanding and making a commitment to the balancing of multiple life roles.

The ever-changing realities of life take each of us on a unique and fascinating journey through various highways, side trips, peaks and valleys, tourist traps, and major attractions. We subscribe to the notion that one's journey though life (career) can be a well-planned trip or a random series of adventures or detours. Schools that are trying to empower youth to take control of their futures are aligned with the former metaphor instead of the latter. In *Lessons for Life,* we introduce each chapter with a sub title that highlights a different part of the career/life journey. Students may need assistance in understanding some of the subtleties and nuances of this metaphor as they participate in the lessons in this book, but the insight into their personal life journey may be one of the most important lessons they will learn during their school years. Well-planned career journeys should help them make sense of their current educational experiences, while assisting them as they focus on their futures.

Obviously, the use of metaphors is not unique to this book. The use of the journey metaphor provides one example of how the *Lessons for Life* curriculum is an *integrated* curriculum. Metaphors can be used in language arts and history classrooms with very little disruption to the normal routine. Many of the lessons in this book could easily be infused in other content areas, as well. For a developmental life skills curriculum to be truly successful, it must be comprehensive—and to be truly comprehensive, we recommend that it be integrated into the regular academic curriculum.

We hope you, too, enjoy your journey through the pages of *Lessons for Life,* especially as you venture out into some of the lesson plans that have been "mapped out" for your use. Keep your eyes on the horizon, as well as the compass, and may all your passengers be happy travelers.

Acknowledgments

We have worked together on a number of projects since 1987, and both have felt compelled to respond to the need for a comprehensive career curriculum that was practical and user-friendly. Writing this book was lots of fun, though. In fact, people would sometimes comment that we seemed to be having too much fun to be writing a book. Along the way, we became increasingly excited as family, colleagues, and students nurtured our efforts.

Bette Ann's husband, Ian, and son, Ian, provided long-standing support and understanding as a myriad of papers covered every flat surface in the house. Daughter Jennifer became integrally involved as the designer of many worksheets and most important as a continual cheerleader (cards, letters, and phone calls greatly appreciated!).

Administrators, staff, and students (including USM interns) at Woolwich Central School who, because of their high standards and high expectations, insisted upon a well-designed, skill-based, practical program will recognize most of the Lessons for Life. Their suggestions for each lesson greatly enhanced their creation and Bette Ann's role as a school counselor.

Zark's wife, Kitty, is a director of guidance, as well as a high school counselor, and has provided a valuable perspective about the challenges facing teenagers. Sons Tygh, Tod, and Kyle, provide a reality base for thinking about the important lessons that need to be included across a broad age range to prepare students for an ever-changing world of work. All four have recognized Zark's need for such creative outlets and have provided much appreciated support and encouragement for this project.

Zark's school counseling students and professional colleagues at USM have been a constant source of ideas, motivation, and resourcefulness. It is inspirational to share in the vision and the challenge of creating quality career curriculum materials that our students can use to empower youth. Their excitement about their chosen profession is infectious. As they have graduated from the program, many students have asked, "When can I get my hands on that book you've been working on?" What really makes creative scholarship such an enjoyable part of Zark's work at the University of Southern Maine is being a part of a counselor education program that is second to none, a department that is "the best," a College of Education and Human Development that operates according to a best practices mentality, and a university that acknowledges one of its core values as a commitment to linking theory to practice.

A special thank you goes to Kerry Bertalan, who has patiently abided our frenzied styles and has meticulously typed, organized, edited, and refined the manuscript, especially in its final stages. We are truly blessed to have her be a part of this effort. She's one in a million!

We also want to acknowledge the creative talents of Wendy Rudolph, who created the cartoon in the Step-by-Step lesson in the elementary volume.

Finally, we would like to acknowledge the support and guidance of Susan Kolwicz, our Acquisitions Editor at The Center for Applied Research in Education, who has always been responsive to our questions, concerns, and anxieties. It was reassuring to work with an editor who listened to the needs of the authors while also attending to the requisite demands of the publishing company.

Our ultimate acknowledgment is to both present and future generations of students. We firmly believe in the adage that children are our future; it is what inspires us to go to work every day and to work on projects like *Lessons for Life.*

Table of Contents

CHAPTER FOUR
In the Driver's Seat
Lessons to Promote Self-Knowledge
27

CHAPTER FIVE
Nice Set o' Wheels
Lessons to Help Students Examine Life Roles
71

CHAPTER SIX
Start Your Engines
Lessons to Promote Educational Development
123

CHAPTER SEVEN
The Roadmap
Lessons to Foster Career Exploration and Planning
181

EPILOGUE
A Look in the Rearview Mirror
Reflections on *Lessons for Life*
227

CHAPTER ONE

Two Roads Diverged ...

A Focus for the *Lessons for Life* Curriculum

In the following scenario, you are witness to a telephone conversation between two high school seniors (stay with us, elementary and middle school folks; there's a message here for you, as well):

> Hi, Kim. I'm glad I caught you before you went to work. You'll never guess who I met while shopping at the mall—Mike Taylor! I hadn't seen him since his family moved to Hicksville in sixth grade. He's just as nice as he was back then, and he suggested we catch up on things over a pizza.
>
> When I told him I was shopping for clothes, he said, "Yah, like who has money for clothes these days?!" So, of course, I told him how I had fallen into the best part-time job while interviewing an accountant for my portfolio activity. He got this strange look on his face and said, "Portfolio? What's that?"
>
> Can you imagine? He had no idea that we'd been working on our career portfolios since about the time he moved six years ago. Weren't we working on them when he was there? Anyway, I told him that over the years, we had been making entries in our portfolios, so that when it came time to make our first real career decisions, we'd have all this great information to draw on ... and now it was really starting to pay off.
>
> You know what he said? "Boy, I wouldn't know where to start." That's pretty sad. So, I told him about all the cooperative learning activities, guest speakers from the community, interviews, family research projects, interest inventories, role plays, and all. He just couldn't believe it.
>
> Remember that assignment we had where we had to write a letter to our unborn child telling about ourselves and our dreams for the baby's future? I told him about that, and he said, "Man, I don't have the foggiest idea about my own future. I've just taken the minimum requirements for graduation and played sports. Football is the only thing I'm really good at, so I'll probably try out for a pro team someday."
>
> You know, Kim, he's a real nice guy, but I'm not sure he has a clue about where he's going and how he's going to get there. I guess with all the stuff we've been exposed to, we seem to have some lessons about life that he's really missed out on."

This scenario could happen in "Anytown," as students who have participated in developmental career guidance programs speak to peers who haven't. Educators have a significant responsibility to assist students in analyzing and synthesizing information about their lives that lead to more purposeful and meaningful careers.

As the scenario suggests, laying the foundation for such important life decisions takes *years* of development and nurturing. Critical skills need to be taught, concepts explored, and options evaluated. The challenge we face as educators is to put these important learning opportunities into some kind of understandable sequence of lessons that will help students grasp their significance and then begin to make the process work for them.

Another chore for busy educators, you say? No, not really. What the above scenario does suggest, more than anything else, is that students really need a career guidance *curriculum—a conceptual framework*—that helps them do the investigating, reflecting, analyzing, and synthesizing so they can see how this interconnected puzzle of school and job and life fits together. You are probably already providing some of these important lessons in your classrooms and group activities. What *Lessons for Life* does is to offer educators a time-efficient resource that addresses the four major competency areas needed for successful life skills and career development—and it provides that conceptual framework that students so desperately need. The addition of *Lessons for Life* to your instructional materials will just complement, "spice up," and give a better context to the excellent things you are already doing.

School counselors often use the term "developmental" to explain the perspective of the guidance and counseling program, to help understand students' needs and behavior at different ages, and to appreciate the progressive nature of the educational process as we work with individuals and groups over several years while they are in school. Our own professional growth as educators is also best represented in a developmental perspective. Just as we do not expect students to be fully empowered to handle life's adjustments, neither can we expect new counselors and teachers to begin their careers with a fully integrated career development curriculum that totally reflects their unique talents and skills. Actually, we don't even have such expectations for "experienced" educators, since the concept of a developmental career guidance curriculum may be new to them, as well. As the metaphor suggests, the curriculum road has diverged in recent years, and a great deal more emphasis is being placed on how schools prepare youth for school-to-work transitions. At the same time, each educator approaches that fork in the road from a developmental perspective that represents her or his unique training, personality, and experience. As teachers and community members become more involved in this career development journey, we must be sensitive to where these people are developmentally, as well. This book of lessons was designed with the career development *program* in mind—while also attending to both the issues of the students who must make those difficult choices about their lives and the educators who will play such critical roles in those decisions. Practitioners are encouraged to use the book and apply its lessons according to their own professional stage of development, constantly striving to nurture their skills and expertise as providers of a quality career guidance curriculum.

Lessons for Life was initially created in response to scores of requests from counselors, teachers, and administrators throughout the United States (and even some foreign countries) who wanted one set of "lessons" that could accompany the *Get a Life* Personal Planning Portfolio, a resource that was cooperatively developed by the American School Counselor Association and the National Occupational Information Coordinating Committee (NOICC). However, it became very apparent in the early stages of development that *Lessons for Life* was going to be equally valuable for counselors and teachers who were not using *Get a Life*. Essentially, it is a resource for educators who embrace the value and significance of a developmental curriculum that focuses on the essential lessons that students need to work through to make good personal, social, educational, and career decisions in their lives.

The *Get a Life* portfolio was created as a prototype model for managing and delivering a comprehensive developmental career guidance program. Because the model recognizes that excellent lessons and practices are already in operation in most schools, it provides a flexible framework for integrating a variety of useful strategies and resources. However, many educators—especially those in the early developmental stages of creating a career development curriculum—expressed frustration at having to draw upon a whole array of resources to address students' self-knowledge, life role understanding, educational development, and career exploration and planning needs. The task just seemed too complex and demanding. *Lessons for Life* started out as a resource for those people who had been saying, "Give me *one* good resource that will help me see how to make this all work!"

Schools know they should have a career guidance curriculum, but who has the time to create one? This book provides the framework and the lessons to assist school counselors, teachers, and other educators as they embark upon the tremendous challenge of creating a career development curriculum that is focused, flexible, and fun.

Lessons for Life is definitely *focused*. It is focused on a comprehensive developmental career guidance program model, while providing separate volumes of lessons at the elementary and secondary school levels. When used accordingly, it can be focused on the topical framework used in the *Get a Life* portfolio, thus creating many opportunities for student reflection and "best work" contributions to their life planning. It is also focused on the National Career Development Guidelines (as was the *Get a Life* portfolio) as a source of content validity. The Guidelines are a nationally validated life-span model of career development, and they provide a well-developed list of competencies that individuals should possess to be successful in a competitive world economy. Essentially, the model helps students focus on the divergent paths they can choose so they make their decisions with their eyes open.

We have also designed *Lessons for Life* to be *flexible*. Several design features acknowledge the importance of educators' adding their own creative touches and addressing the unique needs of the school or community. The format of the lessons allows you to add your own ideas and resources. As your program needs change, your curriculum should reflect those changes, as you refine both the content and the mode of instruction. The comprehensive categories for the lessons provide you with a contextual framework you can use for classifying other lessons you have created to meet the unique needs of your school or classroom. The Notes section on each lesson plan is offered as a place where you can write your own suggestions for improving or changing a lesson—or write reminders about important points to make in the lesson.

You will also note that some of the lessons provide flexibility for creating advanced learning opportunities and extensions of the lessons. Most lessons can be conducted within a typical class period; however, some may be adapted as career guidance units or be extended through homework assignments and community projects. Finally, the lessons are flexible in promoting an integrated curriculum. Teachers in a variety of disciplines will be able to see how the lessons complement their classes' subject matter.

Being focused and flexible is certainly important, but we really wanted *Lessons for Life* to be *fun*. Students will enjoy the creative strategies for discovering their personal strengths, challenges, influences, interests, goals, and opportunities. Even the names of the lessons can be fun for students as they try to figure out why a lesson on self-concept is called "Pass the Roles" or why "Power of the Stars" is the name of a lesson on job-seeking skills. All the lessons try to actively engage students in their own developmental process. The message on the back cover of the *Get a Life* portfolio encourages students to "enjoy a wonderful journey of exploration as you discover who you are and what you want for your future." If they are to enjoy the journey and know the right way to go when the roads diverge, students need to know that much of the reflective and decision-making process can be fun, too.

We hope that your Career Development Curriculum is full of lessons for life. As you develop a curriculum that assists youth in developing the knowledge, skills, and attributes that will empower them in a complex world, we also hope that *Lessons for Life* helps to empower you.

Students talk about their school experiences well after graduation. Students who use *Lessons for Life* will be able to compare notes with students who attended schools that didn't use such lessons and will say that they were able to choose "the road less traveled … and that has made all the difference."

CHAPTER TWO

The Lay of the Land

A Foundation for Understanding *Lessons for Life*

Lessons for Life was designed to focus on practical ideas you can use in classrooms to empower students to make good choices in their lives. However, practical ideas work best when used in the context of a larger framework that provides depth and meaning to those ideas. Continuing the metaphor that one's career is a journey through life, this chapter helps you, the educator, to be a better tour guide by understanding the "lay of the land."

We hesitate to use the words, because we know that some people find this part of a resource to be less exciting and creative than the lessons, but here goes, anyway: This chapter is about theory and philosophy. Now, we realize that you may be tempted to avoid the "theoretical stuff" and turn directly to the lesson plans, but we want to encourage you to resist that temptation so we can share some information that will provide the contextual framework for maximizing those lesson plans. This chapter and the following chapter of practical suggestions provide the larger picture into which these lessons fit. The best tour guides know how to enrich a journey with the special knowledge and insight they have about "what's out there" and what people need or want to know. Educators helping students on their career journey need to provide similar insights.

School-aged students are already in the midst of their own career development, although too often it seems more like haphazard wandering than a trip with a clear destination. Acknowledging that career development is a process, not an event, schools must nurture that development from the first day of kindergarten—when we open children's eyes to the possibilities before them—until students graduate from high school—when they should be focused and excited about embarking upon their future choices and development. To get to this focused time in their lives, students need to be nurtured through stages of awareness, exploration, decision making, and planning. The whole community needs to be involved in students' career development, but the schools must create the structure and the opportunities for aspirations to be realized. The career guidance curriculum is the most feasible means of providing that integrated structure and those opportunities. Since the career guidance curriculum cuts across disciplines and grade levels, students begin to see the interconnectedness of their school experience—the lay of the land.

In the following sections, we are going to share some of the theoretical and philosophical perspectives that undergird a comprehensive career guidance curriculum. These are separate but related paradigms that, when brought together, provide a powerful synergistic model of empowerment for youth. The comprehensive developmental guidance and counseling model is explained because it offers a holistic framework that complements the *Lessons for Life* and *Get a Life* delivery systems. In fact, in some schools, counselors may be the sole proprietors of the comprehensive career guidance curriculum.

Three other broad-based initiatives are also summarized. The National Career Development Guidelines and the SCANS (Secretary's Commission on Achieving Necessary Skills) Competencies are both national models of excellence that were created

5

with all educators in mind—administrators, teachers, counselors, and members of the community. Career development facilitators who want to understand the lay of the land should know something about these significant initiatives, so that future plans and actions are in keeping with the vision of our national leaders.

The last section shares information about the authentic assessment movement, which is a major topic in school reform discussions. The reflective learning model encourages students to claim more ownership of their educational experiences. This concept has significance in that *Lessons for Life* provides opportunities for students to assume more ownership of their own life journeys.

Comprehensive Developmental Guidance and Counseling Programs

For more than two decades, leaders in school counseling have been advocating a comprehensive developmental model, with the concept gaining more refinement and definition as it has matured. While reasons exist why schools have not embraced and implemented comprehensive developmental school counseling and guidance programs, there are no excuses. The following foundational explanation will highlight basic elements of a comprehensive developmental program, but you are encouraged to pursue the more in-depth resources listed at the end of this chapter to develop more knowledge and skills in this area.

What Makes It Comprehensive?

The school counselor's office is often depicted as the place students go to (a) if they have a problem, (b) if they're going to college, or (c) if they need their schedules changed. However, a program that is comprehensive is for *all* students—those in school-to-work programs, gifted and talented individuals, kindergarten students beginning their school careers, students with disabilities and academic challenges, the acting-out child, the star athlete, and the shy individual with hidden talents. *All* students need to have regular access to information, activities, resources, and services as a part of their school experience.

Many statewide models of comprehensive developmental guidance and counseling programs are patterned after the "Missouri Model" developed by Norm Gysbers and associates at the University of Missouri. Briefly stated, the model organizes the program into four major components: guidance curriculum, individual planning, responsive services, and system support (sometimes referred to as program management). Too many school counseling programs spend inordinate amounts of time in the responsive services arena, providing individual and small-group counseling and consultation. There are enough problems that need attention in schools so that counselors could always have more than enough to do just focusing on "putting out fires." However, this is a reactive mode of operation, not a proactive model. A developmental model, on the other hand, tries to minimize reactive services and put most of its energy into preventive efforts. *Lessons for Life* puts its emphasis on the other three areas of the Missouri Model. The combined volumes of *Lessons for Life* provide a systemic model for a comprehensive program. The lesson plans offer a comprehensive guidance curriculum that delivers the content students will need to facilitate their individual planning.

For such a program to be comprehensive, it needs to be *thorough* in addressing a range of topics that meets the needs of all youth in the school. The range of topics needs to reflect students' developmental needs, the community's priorities, and significant state or national initiatives. However, this thoroughness can only be provided with respect to the time, personnel, and resources of each unique setting. Therefore, a systematic way of determining topical priorities should be employed. Essentially, a topical map will help the school "cover the territory," so all the travelers' needs can receive attention and all the major landmarks are seen in perspective.

Last but not least, a comprehensive program needs to include more than just school counselors in the delivery of the program. Teachers, specialists, administrators, parents, community members, and students can all play critical roles in adding depth and substance to the activities and services that make up the program. While the counselors—preferably with an advisory committee—will remain responsible for *managing* how all these people are used, the program will be enriched by involving the whole school and the whole community.

Why Should It Be Developmental?

The guidance and counseling program is the gatekeeper of students' social, educational, and career development while they are in school. Developmental psychology recognizes that there are important challenges, processes, and opportunities that students must address as they experience the various stages of their evolving selves. A quality guidance and counseling program anticipates the basic developmental transitions that students will face and attempts to facilitate those transitions in didactic, nurturing, and supportive ways.

Such a program also recognizes that some students will face greater challenges than others or have circumstances in their lives that serve to thwart their development. For these students, developmental *counseling* is needed to help put them back on track as quickly as possible and to avoid further complications. This is where the responsive services component of the total program is seen in perspective.

To efficiently serve the developmental needs of *all* students, a guidance curriculum needs to be created that identifies the developmental topics or issues that are critical for student development and the most appropriate grade levels at which the topics should be addressed. According to Robert Myrick, a noted authority on developmental guidance and counseling programs, "developmental guidance and counseling assumes that human nature moves individuals sequentially and positively toward self-enhancement."

In the "life as a journey" metaphor used in this book, the developmental aspect of the program tries to determine the itinerary and the major "stops" along the way. Developmentalists need to be attuned to when "rest stops" may be needed, as well.

What's the Difference between Guidance and Counseling?

Those of you who are trying to understand this model for the first time may be wondering why both the terms guidance and counseling are used in describing the program. The term *guidance* has been called vague, confusing, and archaic by some authors in the field. However, others (including the authors of this book) prefer to retain the term, since including such activities or services as career fairs, group test interpretations, public relations initiatives, and computer searches under *school coun-*

seling is both confusing and misleading. For the purposes of assisting educators with the *Lessons for Life* curriculum, the following definitions will be used:

> *Counseling:* Counseling relationships are defined as ongoing helping processes, confidential in nature, that assist people in focusing on personal concerns, planning strategies to address specific issues, and evaluating their success in carrying out these plans. Successful counseling relationships require a high level of knowledge about human development and behavior, as well as effective and facilitative communication skills.
>
> *Developmental Guidance:* This ecnompasses schoolwide activities and services designed to help students focus on the attainment of knowledge and skills for developing healthy life goals and acquiring the behaviors to reach those goals. In elementary, middle, and high schools, these developmental services are aimed at helping students focus on tasks and issues appropriate for their age and stage of life.

How Is It a Program?

Too many school counselors have a conglomeration of services and activities without having a program. Such situations usually result in the counselors being misunderstood and unappreciated. Program management skills are necessary to properly initiate, integrate, articulate, implement, and be accountable for a well-rounded and well-run program. There needs to be a systemic unity to all the components of the program. Unless all the key players are in agreement on the conceptual framework of the program and are able to adequately explain the program to students, colleagues, superiors, and the public, very little support will be generated to nurture the program's development. This is an area where counselors need to have a perspective on the lay of the land for their own programs and their own school districts, so they can more effectively tell others where they are coming from, where they are now, and where they are going.

Educators using the *Lessons for Life* materials should examine the resources in light of the existing program in the school. If it is not understood how lessons will complement the school's mission and the guidance and counseling program's goals, then time should be devoted to engaging people in a discussion about these important issues. If no leadership is being provided in the area of guidance program management, then action steps should be taken to assure that *someone* in a leadership position takes coursework or in-service training, reads current literature, or receives consultation assistance to gain these important skills.

THE GUIDANCE CURRICULUM

While all aspects of a comprehensive developmental school guidance and counseling program are important, the guidance curriculum is at the very heart of the program. Without it, counselors are seen merely as providing a conglomeration of services. The guidance curriculum is the vehicle for *delivering* a program that is truly comprehensive and developmental. The guidance curriculum is also seen as an integral part of the total school's curriculum, not as an add-on. As much as possible, the guidance curriculum should be integrated with subject area curricula so that students can see the interrelationships in their learning and the practical applications of the guidance lessons.

If, in assessing the lay of the land in your district, you discover that there is no guidance curriculum, then *Lessons for Life* can help you decide what is needed in your school to address students' developmental needs in the areas of self-knowledge, life roles, educational development, and career exploration and planning. However, if your school does have a guidance curriculum, the task at hand is to review that curriculum to see if "the whole territory" is being covered or whether there are some blank spots on the map. If you're lucky, you may find that your school is doing everything it should be doing. In such a case, put on the cruise control and enjoy the scenery!

Just as "seeing the big picture" is important in the total management of the guidance and counseling program, this same kind of broad visioning is also valued in curriculum development. According to Allan Glatthorn, writing in a publication of the Association for Supervision and Curriculum Development, there are four major considerations in gaining a good grasp of the big picture:

(a) *Knowing what elements will shape your work.* Keep in mind national, state, and local guidelines and initiatives. The National Career Development Guidelines and the SCANS Report, mentioned later in this chapter, are examples of the kinds of elements that might shape a larger vision of a comprehensive and substantive curriculum.

(b) *Knowing specifically what you will produce.* A good curriculum should operate according to a mutually agreed-upon list of goals and topics, a scope-and-sequence framework that targets grade levels and order of presentation, and a list of materials that will assist in the delivery.

(c) *Understanding who will carry out the tasks.* Both the responsibilities for overseeing the total curriculum and the identification of individuals who will actually deliver its lessons require careful thought and attention. Both management and implementation factors are at work here, but the key question should be "Who can be most effective in helping students learn these important lessons?" It may be that a teacher, a parent, a community member, a school custodian, or a peer helper might be the most resourceful or persuasive individual for facilitating particular lessons. However, all participants need to be aware of their responsibilities and they must be able to plan accordingly, so managing assignments is a crucial need.

(d) *Identifying what needs to be done to carry out the tasks.* Staff development, selection of textbooks (or integrated curriculum handbooks), and decisions about authentic assessment of the curriculum and student competencies are critical aspects of being accountable to a quality curriculum. Decisions in these areas should be made in the context of existing plans and procedures within a school system. Educators using *Lessons for Life* should also view these three areas of accountability as critical factors for successfully transitioning to a new and more fully integrated curriculum that is complementary to other programs.

The *Lessons for Life* curriculum materials should be used in the context of this big picture framework. Because flexibility has been built into the lessons, educators can adapt and adopt lessons according to local needs or national guidelines, according to the scope and sequence plan of an individual teacher or an entire district, and according to the unique talents or preferences of those who will be delivering the lessons. However, everyone should be operating from the same basic map.

NATIONAL MODELS OF EXCELLENCE

Some schools like to use national models of excellence to establish the "content validity" of their work. (Remember that concept from your research class?) Since two such models were used by the American School Counselor Association in the development of the *Get a Life* portfolio, and because they are in keeping with the comprehensive developmental model that was just explained, they are offered here as examples of how theoretical frameworks can provide more credibility for a program's efforts. The National Career Development Guidelines and the SCANS competencies are holistic models that have been well received by the lay public and legislative bodies alike.

National Career Development Guidelines

During the 1980s, a cadre of national leaders in various career development groups joined forces to create the National Career Development (NCD) Guidelines (National Occupational Information Coordinating Committee, 1988), identifying the competencies needed to be successful in a global economy and society. The Guidelines are seen as a *complement* to a comprehensive developmental program, rather than as a conflicting model. Essentially, the Guidelines provide a well-grounded framework for a comprehensive program, and they are especially appealing to administrators, school board members, and parents because they provide a practical, commonsense, and understandable approach to empowering youth. The *Get a Life* portfolio was created to demonstrate the compatibility of the comprehensive developmental school counseling and guidance program model and the National Career Development Guidelines, and to provide a tangible resource for schools to use in assisting youth with the development of their career competencies.

As a national model, the National Career Development Guidelines offer schools a "*way* of the land." At least eight national associations have endorsed the NCD Guidelines, recommending that they be used for creating high-quality programs. The guidelines provide hierarchically arranged competencies at the elementary school, middle school, high school, and adult levels, illustrating that career development is a lifelong venture. As stated in the introduction to the Guidelines, "they provide a blueprint of career development competencies that children, youth, and adults should master, and identify standards or indicators of evidence that individuals have attained those competencies."

Schools do not have to accept the National Career Development Guidelines as the only acceptable model, but counselors, students, parents, and the community should commit themselves to some model of career development. The message to students needs to be clear: Career development is not just about "getting jobs"; it's about "getting a life!" A holistic, balanced perspective on life (one's ultimate career) development is what every school should be aspiring to promote as one of its major goals.

Most career development models advocate a three-dimensional paradigm for emphasizing Self-Knowledge, Educational Development, and Occupational Exploration and Planning as interconnected components of the broader concept of one's career. The *Get a Life* portfolio model used some editorial license to incorporate several important topics from those three components into a fourth area called "Life Roles," thus emphasizing the critical importance of such factors as family aspirations, cultural heritage, sex-role stereotyping, and peer influences in nurturing or limiting one's career development. These three (or four) categories can provide an organizational and conceptual framework for a school's guidance curriculum. It becomes obvious in this book that this four-part framework was the organizational scheme for the *Lessons for Life* curriculum.

The SCANS Report

During the early 1990s, the Secretary's Commission on Achieving Necessary Skills (SCANS) was directed to advise the U.S. Secretary of Labor on the level of skills required for young people to meet the demands of a global economy and a workforce that was increasingly dependent on technology. The commission explored the current situation and future needs in American schools and the American workplace through extensive discussions, interviews, and meetings with business owners, public employers, unions, and workers and supervisors in shops, plants, and stores. The prevailing message from their research was:

> Good jobs will increasingly depend on people who can put knowledge to work. What we found was disturbing: more than half our young people leave school without the knowledge or foundation required to find and hold a good job. These young people will pay a very high price. They face the bleak prospects of dead-end work interrupted only by periods of unemployment. (SCANS, 1992, p. xv)

The message was not intended so much as a portent of doom but as a call to action. This was a "wake-up call" to schools and communities and governments to take responsible steps to reform educational systems so that students could be prepared for the demands of the twenty-first century. As one becomes familiar with the lay of the land, it becomes obvious that the "way" of the land is to become more aware of the "way of the world." The SCANS Report became a significant document in influencing future legislation and national and state initiatives to make education more relevant to students' and communities' and the nation's needs. You will find the language of the SCANS Report infused in many of the school reform documents generated by state legislatures and departments of education during the past few years, as well as federal legislation like the School-to-Work Opportunities Act of 1994.

A major recommendation of the SCANS Report was that schools find ways to promote "workplace know-how" which would lead to effective job performance. This know-how has two elements: competencies and a foundation. The report advocated that five major competencies and a three-part foundation of skills and personal qualities be "taught and understood in an integrated fashion that reflects the workplace *contexts* in which they are applied" (p. xv). In other words, the commission recommended that learning take place within the real environment, as much as possible, instead of operating within an abstract framework that students could not fully appreciate.

The five major SCANS competencies are in the areas of Resources (identifies, organizes, plans, and allocates resources); Interpersonal (works with others); Information (acquires and uses information); Systems (understands complex interrelationships); and Technology (works with a variety of technologies). Careful examination will reveal that many of the competencies are already a part of most schools' curricula. For example, under the Information section students should be able to "interpret and communicate information"—certainly an integral aspect of most language arts programs. Other competencies are very commonsense, practical items that probably *should* be part of every curriculum, but perhaps are not. Under the Interpersonal section, for example, the SCANS competencies suggest that all students should be able to "negotiate—work toward agreements involving exchange of resources; resolves divergent interests." Still other competencies reflect the technological, global diversity, and economic realities of our changing world and must be infused in curricula to help students succeed in life.

The three-part foundation explained in the SCANS document addresses Basic Skills (reading, writing, listening, mathematics, and speaking), Thinking Skills (creative thinking, problem solving, decision making, knowing how to learn, seeing with the mind's eye, and reasoning), and Personal Qualities (responsibility, self-esteem, sociability, self-management, and integrity/honesty). While the first area (Basic Skills) is often the focus of the school's curriculum, the SCANS Report emphasized that the thinking skills and personal qualities also needed increased attention if students were to be prepared to work in a high-performance workplace.

The *Get a Life* portfolio includes many items from the SCANS competencies and three-part foundation, demonstrating that these important aspects of Self-Knowledge are an integral part of one's career development. As a result, *Lessons for Life* includes several lesson plans for helping students explore their own competence in these areas.

REFLECTIVE LEARNERS/PRODUCTIVE EARNERS

Authentic assessment is one of the current buzzwords in the educational reform movement. Authentic assessment goes beyond performance assessment in that students not only complete or demonstrate a desired behavior, but they do so in the context of real-life applications. There are several complex facets of authenticity—such as task complexity, motivation, locus of control, and criteria standards—that might be considered which suggest that it is a higher order of applied assessment and that it requires careful deliberation and execution if it is to be used effectively with students.

Portfolios are types of authentic assessment that recognize that norm-referenced tests and imposed standards are insufficient measures for the very significant personal learning that is required for students to truly value the learning process. Portfolios tap into an "internal accountability" process that encourages students, teachers, families, and even community members to think hard about the essential learning that helps individuals to make sense of their world (get the lay of the land) and to think about what evidence can be provided to demonstrate progress and success.

It is easy to see why portfolios are becoming increasingly popular in today's schools. Educators can certainly use the *Lessons for Life* curriculum materials independently of the portfolio model; however, portfolios should be considered as a viable option in providing learning experiences that are more comprehensive and attentive to developmental growth, personal discovery, and empowerment. Part of those learning experiences must include assessment that is more authentic and significant for "personal meaning-making."

Essentially, the portfolio becomes a vehicle for students to reflect upon learning experiences according to their own life experiences and perspectives. If they are encouraged to put their best thinking and best work into the portfolio, it becomes a conduit and receptacle for the significant pieces of work that define their standards and levels of meaning. As reflective learners, they begin to appreciate the need to refine their thinking, their writing, and their contributions to the portfolio.

Since the lesson plans in *Lessons for Life* were created to accompany a nationally validated career (life) development portfolio model, students should have many insights and questions and decisions to reflect upon as they examine who they are and what they want for themselves. By developmentally sequencing lessons in the areas of Self-Knowledge, Life Roles, Educational Development, and Career Exploration and Planning, schools can be instrumental in shaping the "internal accountability" that will assist youth in some of the most significant decision making of their lives. Certainly, one of our goals is to produce *productive earners* in a global economy; however, we also want to produce *reflective learners* who know how to attach their own standards of meaning to the significant questions they will face in life. The lessons in this book applied to a portfolio model can provide a wonderful vehicle for empowering youth to become both reflective learners and productive earners—and in the process, offer a model for learning that can last a lifetime. As travelers on life's journey, they will have more security in moving from one destination to the next because they will have the "lay of the land."

SUMMARY

In this chapter, we have tried to summarize some of the foundational or conceptual underpinnings of the *Lessons for Life* curriculum materials. An appreciation for the evolving significance of these models and guidelines can lend perspective to the rationale behind the lessons in this book and, more important, to the roles you can play in helping youth set an agenda for career/life planning that is personally meaningful and rewarding.

"Seeing the big picture" is only part of the process. Effective educators use such a broad conceptual framework to create their own meaning-making so they can, in turn, interpret the big picture in enlightening and facilitative ways and the students benefit from their vision. Those who truly see the big picture also recognize that as educators we must be role models, reflective learners ourselves in the midst of our own "process." Therefore, it is hoped that some of this information will trigger questions and further investigation in the areas of career guidance program management, career development, guidance curriculum planning, and authentic assessment. As tour guides for the trip of a lifetime, your own adventures should provide you with more than enough insights about what the landscape really looks like.

REFERENCES

Baker, S. B. *School Counseling for the Twenty-First Century.* New York: Merrill, 1992.

Glatthorn, A. A. *Developing a Quality Curriculum.* Alexandria, VA: ASCD, 1994.

Gysbers, N. C. & Henderson, P. *Developing and Managing Your School Guidance Program.* Alexandria, VA: ACA, 1988.

Meyer, C. A. "What's the difference between authentic and performance assessment?" *Educational Leadership,* May 1992: 39-40.

Myrick, R. D. *Developmental Guidance and Counseling: A Practical Approach* (2nd edition). Minneapolis: Educational Media, 1993.

NOICC. *National Career Development Guidelines.* Washington, DC: National Occupational Information Coordinating Committee (NOICC), 1989; 1996.

Schmidt, J. J. *Counseling in Schools: Essential Services and Comprehensive Programs.* Boston: Allyn & Bacon, 1993.

School-to-Work Opportunities Act of 1994, 20 U.S.C.A. § 6111 et seq.

Secretary's Commission on Achieving Necessary Skills. *What Work Requires of Schools: A SCANS Report for America 2000.* Washington, DC: U.S. Department of Labor, 1991.

VanZandt, C. E. & Hayslip, J. B. *Your Comprehensive School Guidance and Counseling Program: A Handbook of Practical Activities.* New York: Longman, 1994.

VanZandt, C. E., Perry, N. S., & Brawley, K. T. *Get a Life: Your Personal Planning Portfolio for career Development.* Alexandria, VA: ASCA, 1993.

Wolf, D. P., LeMahieu, P. G., & Eresh, J. "Good Measure: Assessment as a tool for educational reform." *Educational Leadership,* May, 1992: 8-13.

CHAPTER THREE

Planning the Trip

Practical Tips for Settings Things in Motion

Because the lessons in this book represent a departure from the more traditional delivery systems and focus more on a preventive and integrated approach to empowering youth, we want to share a few suggestions and considerations that may assist you in organizing and delivering the lessons. These practical issues are mostly common sense, but are worth repeating because of their significance in fostering the success of your program. Even though you may have taken this trip before, it is always a good idea to check your plans to make sure you have not forgotten anything.

In the deliberations about how things get done, the students and their needs are central to all our planning. This chapter on management issues starts with the larger mission in mind, then proceeds to the more specific needs of instructors and individual students. This systemic perspective highlights the importance of everyone following the same map so that people don't get lost along the way.

The first section focuses on management issues that relate to both school politics and program delivery. The second section attends to classroom issues and provides information, techniques, and suggestions for enhancing the learning experiences of students as they participate in the *Lessons for Life* curriculum. Finally, we offer a few notes about student concerns that may surface as they participate in cooperative learning experiences and become more adept at being reflective learners.

These practical suggestions are offered in a snapshot format so that you can quickly scan the entire chapter to get a sense of the variety of concerns that need to be considered in planning and delivering a quality career guidance curriculum. You are encouraged to pursue more in-depth reading on topics that are of particular concern to you.

Management Issues

Administrative Support

Know the people who can act on your behalf when questions are asked and decisions are made about program priorities, resource allocations, and budget requests. Successful programs recognize the importance of administrative support and involvement. In business, employees wouldn't (or shouldn't, anyway) plan trips without management recognizing how the trips support the company's mission. The trips often carry more significance, as well, if the CEO goes along on the junket. The same thinking holds true in schools.

Involve the Principal. Your key ally in promoting curricular change in a building is the school's administrator. Educate your principal about *Lessons for Life*. Show how this curriculum complements the school's curriculum. Reinforce how attention to students' developmental needs can promote better learning. Keep your principal informed so he or she can address faculty and community concerns as knowledgeably as the counselor or the coordinator of the *Lessons for Life* curriculum. (Principals hate to be caught off-guard. Can you blame them?)

Keep District Administrators Informed.   If you have a Curriculum Coordinator, work closely with that person to build support for the career guidance curriculum and to make sure *Lessons for Life* materials are aligned with district guidelines. If your district does not have a Curriculum Coordinator, be sure to work with your principal to apprise the superintendent of any curricular changes you make.

Appreciate the Power of School Boards.   Recognize that with all the decisions school board members have to make (as volunteers), they need concise, informative communication to help them understand why your program is important. At least twice a year, update them on the success of your program.

Create an Advisory Committee.   Choose active members of the school and community who can offer ideas, feedback, and perspective, while also sharing their enthusiasm for the curriculum and/or the guidance and counseling program, if that is where *Lessons for Life* will be the focus. Meet three or four times a year. Strike a balance between asking them to do too much and having them "rubber stamp" everything you tell them you are doing. Advisory committee members can be some of the best spokespersons for your program.

Public Relations

Most people only see small snippets of your curriculum or program and draw conclusions about its worth and effectiveness based on that inadequate information. You must find a way to creatively, concisely, coherently, and correctly portray both your goals and your accomplishments. The school year only allows time for about three or four major PR projects, so choose the ones that will maximize your message!

Use Informational Letters to Parents.   An introductory letter that explains the new *Lessons for Life* curriculum should include the benefits and purposes, as well as examples of some of the lessons. If your school is using the *Get a Life* portfolio, this would also be a good time to introduce it. Later, letters like the one accompanying the "What's in a Name?" lesson (in the Life Roles section) may be sent home to encourage parent involvement in learning activities.

Promote Community Networking.   There are a variety of ways to involve the community. Some of the lessons encourage students to talk with community members. Set the stage for such involvement by meeting with groups like the Chamber of Commerce or local service clubs to discuss community-based learning opportunities. Agree to speak at luncheons or meetings where you can give an overview of the curriculum, show examples of how students are involved in their career development, and seek volunteers who would like to contribute their time or resources.

Press for Media Coverage.   Use local cable or network television and radio stations, as well as newspapers, to illustrate the highlights of your program. Share some good news for a change. Invite students and community members to be a part of the press coverage.

Offer Interesting Events. Use National School Counseling Week, a Career Fair, the National Career Development Month Poster Contest, Aspirations Day, or some other event to showcase some of the special features of your program or curriculum. Invite or include parents and the public.

Logistical Planning

Just as a long family automobile trip is usually more successful if you have an itinerary, a good roadmap, a well-tuned and comfortable car, good drivers, and a cooperative family, a successful curriculum requires similar features. Attention to critical logistical matters can help make the transition to a new curriculum run a lot more smoothly.

Create a Scope-and-Sequence Chart. Visually outline the grade and time of year that various topics or lessons will be offered. This will help school board members, administrators, teachers, and parents see the "big picture" more clearly. It will also help those who are implementing the curriculum to be better organized and focused. If all topics or lessons are not going to be used, this is the time to decide which ones will be omitted (and why).

Conduct In-Service Training. Adjusting to a new curriculum is a developmental process. In the early stages, teachers (and any others who will be implementing the curriculum) will need a broad overview of the total curriculum and where the changes are taking place, a rationale for why the change is important, information about resources, expectations, and responsibilities, and as much as possible, practical activities that familiarize them with the lessons and materials. Conduct in-service training for administrators, as well, to keep them up-to-date and knowledgeable. Last but not least, properly train volunteers so that they understand the school's expectations and the parameters of their responsibilities, and make sure they have the resources, knowledge, and skills to do a good job.

Develop a Schedule. Anybody and everybody who is involved in this curriculum needs to know who does what and when! Share the responsibility, but coordinate the lessons so that conflicts are avoided and learning opportunities are optimized.

Plan Ahead. Develop a master list of supplies, library resources, room assignments, community contacts, guest speakers, A-V equipment, etc., that will be needed by those implementing the curriculum. If individuals are given the responsibility for addressing these considerations on their own, create a grid sheet that all can use to organize their planning in a similar fashion. The librarians, technicians, guest speakers, etc., will appreciate uniform practices. If supplies or materials need to be included in the annual budget, this advanced planning can help delineate program needs and priorities.

Accountability

Parents, administrators, faculty, school board members, students, and interested community members are either curious or concerned about whether change has been worth it. The quality of accountability information is much more important than its quantity.

Collect Evaluation Information.   Both quantitative and qualitative evaluations can assess the effectiveness or support for your program or curriculum. Determine what you think your accountability audiences would like to know (ask them), then create methods for gathering the information. Use local colleges and universities as resources if this seems a formidable task.

Conduct a Needs Assessment.   You could use the advisory committee or a sample of students, teachers, or parents to determine whether the curriculum needs to address other topics that are not currently covered. Compare this information with the evaluation data.

Carry Out Research.   Again, involve your local college professors or research centers to help with this need if research is not your forte. Remember that good research data can be a powerful tool for demonstrating both needs and results.

Involve Advisory Committee in Program Review.   One of the greatest ways an advisory committee can assist a program is to seek information and clarify issues that reflect the year's progress in meeting program goals. Advisory committee members can (a) analyze evaluation and needs assessment data, (b) integrate needs assessment information with other input and materials presented to them, and (c) offer their concerns, commendations, and recommendations for fostering better programming and meeting more needs.

Submit an Annual Report.   As concisely as possible, summarize the year, give examples of successes and problems, list concise evaluative data, make conclusions and recommendations—and as much as possible, *blow your own horn*!

Storage and Retrieval

One of the "most-asked" questions about portfolios is where they should be stored. There is no single best place to keep such materials because every school's situation is unique. Much depends on the space and resources available in individual schools. The materials needed for the *Lessons for Life* curriculum present similar challenges. The important thing for your school is that you recognize the need to address the problem, brainstorm some possible solutions, decide on the best plan in terms of its efficiency and accommodation of needs, then put the plan into practice.

Classroom Issues

Readiness

The foundation for presenting anything new to people is to create a level of readiness that makes them feel secure in that change. If students see *Lessons for Life* (or the *Get a Life* portfolio if you are using it) as something new and exciting, they will anticipate the change with wonder. Planning a trip shouldn't be a drudgery. It should help the travelers look forward to the journey with high expectations.

Create a "Build-Up" That Gets Students Excited.   Start early (even during the previous spring) and use bulletin boards, school newsletters, PA announcements,

T-shirts, displays, etc., to give "sound bytes" that tantalize students about the upcoming curriculum (e.g., "Got a life? Get one next fall!" … or … "Life-altering changes next fall!"). Lay the foundation for this curriculum being something special—and fun.

Help Students See The "Big Picture."   As you explain the *Lessons for Life* curriculum to students, demonstrate its relevance to their lives, the needs of the local community, the economic outlook of your state, national agendas, and the global economy. Also, link the curriculum to their K-12 educational process and to your school's integrated curriculum (if you have one, of course).

Emphasize That Career Is a Process, Not an Event.   "What do you want to be when you grow up?" is one of those (inappropriate) questions that assumes there is one perfect job to which individuals should aspire and they should figure out what it is when they're young. The reality is that people usually make several major career changes in their lives, so a *process* of making career decisions is much more important than finalizing one's choice. One's career is also a process of integrating a job "career" with family, social, leisure, spiritual, and community "careers." Since one's career is a complex process of human development, it should not be viewed as a simplistic decision.

Explain *Lessons for Life* As a Total Package.   Let students explore the meaning of the package of lessons they are being offered as a part of the career guidance curriculum. Although the lessons are designed so they can be used independently of or as a complement to the *Get a Life* portfolio, explaining how the lessons fit together as a group of activities that will help students make more sense out of their lives is an important message.

Teaching and Learning

Learning can certainly take place in the absence of teaching, but learning is enhanced by good teaching. Therefore, we'd like to share some lessons of teaching that may assist those who may be new to the process of facilitating student learning.

Model Instructor/Facilitator Enthusiasm for the Lessons.   So much of what we communicate is nonverbal; therefore, we need to project messages to students that say "This lesson is important." By sharing personal anecdotes that relate to the lessons, teachers are able to demonstrate how personal decision making was (or could have been) a critical aspect of their own development. In the process, students understand the lessons' relevancy.

Reinforce Rules of Group Behavior.   Come to a consensus of group rules (e.g., no put-downs, okay to "pass," etc.) and post them on the chalkboard or bulletin board. Refer to the rules as guidelines for both classroom and small-group behavior.

Be Sure That Lessons Are Understood and Supplies Are in Place.   A very good lesson can come unravelled if poor directions or missing materials keep students from having "all the parts of the puzzle." A five-minute readiness check can help focus the lesson.

Share the Lesson Objectives.   Don't keep the objectives of your lessons a secret. It's okay to let students guess what they think the objectives were after the lesson (a quick evaluation device) as long as they aren't kept in the dark about the abilities they should be able to demonstrate as the result of a lesson.

Don't Bite Off More Than Kids Can Chew.   In our experiences with teachers using the *Get a Life* portfolio for the first time, we've seen many try to have their students fill in an entire *page* of the portfolio in one 45-minute class! Sometimes 45 minutes won't be enough time to fill in a single *frame* on the page because the topic or issue is too complex for students to comprehend, ponder, write about, share, reflect upon, revise, commit to, and rewrite. A combination of professional expertise and common sense will help you determine whether students are developmentally ready to handle the complexities of a lesson. A significant value of portfolio work is the gift of time it gives students to reflect upon the experiences, and to process the information prior to making a final entry.

Make Directions Understandable.   New teachers usually need to read verbatim directions when introducing an exercise to make sure they don't miss anything. Nothing wrong with that! With lesson familiarity, you may develop a more natural delivery and be able to explain the directions instead of reading them. Whatever your comfort level, the important thing to keep in mind is that students must clearly understand what it is they are to do.

Be Flexible.   We mentioned flexibility as one of the trademarks of *Lessons for Life*. Try the lessons once and then decide whether or not you want to add your own flair to an exercise, or adapt it in a particular way that will more effectively meet students' needs or more appropriately reflect your style of teaching. We encourage you to make notes on the lesson plans for future reference.

Reinforce Earlier Lessons.   It may be necessary to remind students of lessons they had previously that can serve as a foundation for a current lesson. Don't assume that all students will see the connections among lessons. Lessons that were particularly fun and/or successful can be especially powerful in getting across fundamental concepts that can enhance a new lesson.

Nurture the Art of Questioning.   In reflective learning, students are encouraged to ponder questions that help them sort out their own levels of meaning and insight. Genuine questioning is at the core of learning, so students need to feel that their questions are valued—both by the instructors and their peers. An atmosphere of acceptance needs to be fostered so that all students feel comfortable asking either basic or profound questions whose answers lead to greater understanding.

Create a Sense of Closure to Lessons.   Spending a few structured moments at the end of each lesson helps most students to put the learning in perspective. The closure questions in *Lessons for Life* allow you to develop this focus. If time runs out at the end of a lesson, be sure to review the lesson in the next session with the class to make sure they have really captured the basic objectives of the lesson. Closure is also helpful in getting students ready to make the transition to more didactic (and less personal) lessons in their next class.

Build in Time for Reflection and Making Entries in the Portfolios. If portfolio entries are supposed to represent the students' best thinking and best work, then sufficient time must be devoted to the process of reflection and refining one's work. While some of this reflection and refinement may be done outside class, teachers should try occasionally to observe the process in class, as well. As both an informal assessment and a reality check, teachers can learn much from the way students address the reflective learning process.

Recognize the "Teachable Moments." Because students bring their unique lives to the learning process, it is imperative that we tune in to the topics, activities, discussions, and questions that capture their fascination, cause wonderment, or motivate them in some way to learn or explore for their own sake. The signs are sometimes subtle (a furrowed eyebrow or leaning forward in a chair) or they might be as obvious as the hands-in-the-air "Ah-hah" gestures or an excited smile, but a good teacher recognizes the need to foster the teachable moment with genuine interest and reinforcement, and sees the possibility of new learning being attached to this moment. There will also be times when it becomes obvious that an entire class is captivated in a teachable moment and the teacher seizes the moment and runs with it—and prays that there will be many more days like this!

Learn from Minor Disasters. There may be times when the very best of lessons "backfire." In such situations, the lesson needs to be analyzed from different points of view. The content, dynamics of the class, the delivery, other events taking place in school, environmental factors, or the basic "chemistry" of the classroom should all be considered in trying to determine why things did not work this time.

Cooperative Learning Foundation

Cooperative learning is the preferred model for *Lessons for Life.* Much can be gained from the interactions of youth as they share their insights, aspirations, questions, and needs. Although the lessons can be adapted to fit the instructor's style, we offer the following highlights of cooperative learning for those who may be unfamiliar with the technique and want to try it out.

Teach Group Process Techniques As the Framework for Cooperative Learning. Whole courses are taught on group process skills, but the following are the basics to which school students should attend.

- *Team-building*—Create activities that allow group members to appreciate individual strengths and needs in the small groups. Foster collaboration versus competition. Plan team-building activities that fit the developmental needs of students. A frivolous hand-holding exercise may be fine for younger students, but the older ones may find it too "touchy-feely" and immature. Two or three team-building activities may be needed before group members begin to recognize each other's strengths and contributions to the team's work.

- *Stages of groups*—Common names for the developmental stages of groups are Forming, Storming, Norming, and Performing (and eventually Adjourning). In the second stage, appreciating that the group *should* experience some frustration, confusion, and disorientation as ideas and questions are shared and goals are defined is reassuring to both students and facilitators. The key to moving successfully through the storming stage is using good communication skills. The most important communication skill is listening. Task-oriented individuals often struggle with this stage because they become impatient with the group spending so much time on understanding each other. The instructor needs to encourage and model patience with the process as the group eventually moves to wonderful levels of creativity and productivity *if* they stay focused and they make sure all group members are included and valued.

- *Leadership in groups*—Every group should have a leader who is assigned or elected. Shared leadership rarely works. Having a designated leader gives one person some permission to move the group toward its goal without seeming too pushy. The group may even want to talk about the kind of leader or leadership they want to help them be successful.

- *Roles students play*—Every group member plays one or more roles in the group. Without leadership or direction, some of the unwanted roles might be joker, shirker, loafer, devil's advocate, troublemaker, pain-in-the-neck … you get the idea! The "Understanding Roles" lessons in the Life Roles section of *Lessons for Life* focuses on the positive roles students can play in group situations. It is often helpful in cooperative learning groups to have members discuss the various roles that will be necessary for their group to be successful, then have members assume responsibility for playing those necessary roles as the group works together.

- *Norms*—Get the groups to list a few basic rules or guidelines that will help them work well together and accomplish their tasks. For example, "no name calling," "respect others' ideas," and "do your best work" are the kinds of norms that often surface. If the norms are posted near where the group works, the leaders or instructors can refer to the list when a group starts to wander from its norms. A basic, manageable list is better than a lengthy one.

Establish an Environment of Trust.   Beyond the basics of group process skills, students also need to trust that the cooperative learning process will work and that they can trust their classmates to be considerate of their needs and individuality. Simple looks or statements can destroy trust. Some of the "Interpersonal Skills" lessons in the Self-Knowledge section discuss the importance of good communication skills, which are key factors in building trust.

Specify and Clarify Group Tasks.   What seems clear to some will appear confusing to others. It's just the nature of things. If lessons call for specific tasks to be accomplished, make sure students fully understand what is expected. Promote questioning as an important part of communicating and understanding. If everyone in the group operates according to the same understanding, then more cohesiveness and cooperation will follow.

Process the Process.   At the very heart of the cooperative learning model is the notion that students need time to reflect on their learning. The process of self-discovery, the process of career decision making, the process of learning in groups, the process of analyzing the depth and meaning of a lesson—all require time and a process for "personal meaning-making." Two of the more obvious ways to accomplish this "processing" are through individual reflection (such as making entries in a journal, in a portfolio, or on a worksheet) and group discussion. By sharing and asking questions in groups, students broaden their perspective on issues, learn a more expansive vocabulary to apply to their life development, and benefit from a kind of "spectator therapy," whereby they learn from the insights and discoveries of others. A strong foundation of group process skills makes "processing the process" a natural extension of the *Lessons for Life* exercises.

Classroom Discipline

The primary ingredient of strong classroom discipline is an exciting curriculum that makes learning fun, relevant, and attainable. We also recognize that the strongest curriculum and the most gifted instructors will still encounter discipline problems on occasion. Our advice is to (a) remain respectful to all; (b) refer to agreed-upon and posted rules; (c) model problem-solving or conflict-resolution skills, if applicable; (d) place reasonable limits on behavior and state your expectations for acceptable behavior; and (e) ask that any student who cannot comply with those limits be removed until willing to comply with expected norms.

When a lesson appears to be going "downhill," we encourage teachers to set the plans aside and analyze the situation with the class. Simply asking, "What seems to be happening here?" may lead to an answer or an awareness that allows the lesson to continue—or to be postponed to address a more timely issue.

Homework Assignments

Several of the lessons in this book include homework assignments that complement or serve as extensions of those lessons. Homework doesn't have to be (and shouldn't be) a drudgery. The following are key aspects of using homework with *Lessons for Life*.

Involve the Parents. Parents and family members are often the most influential people in students' career decisions. The homework assignments are designed to let family members and significant adults share important lessons they have learned about the world of work, what's important in life, and what mistakes to avoid. There are also opportunities to share cultural and ethnic customs and unique perspectives that are so much a part of an individual's development.

See the Community As a Classroom. Students need a view of the real world and the local community provides concrete realities and practical opportunities, as well as abstract possibilities about the world of career development. Homework assignments that encourage youth to learn from their communities also promote a better understanding of the communities as a result of their investigations.

Timing and Workload. If homework assignments from *Lessons for Life* are tacked on to students' workloads when they already have a long list of papers, exams, and projects for which they must study, they may see the assignments as just one more burden of being a student. Allowing ample time for assignments and being attentive to other important class projects, athletic events, vacations, and extracurricular activities will help students be more receptive to the lessons and, in turn, model the significance of striking a balance in one's life among the various roles we must play.

When assignments are continually late, it might behoove the teacher or counselor to ask the student to conference privately. Family situations, jobs, and personal problems are often very legitimate excuses for late work. Ask the student to figure out a plan to get the work done. A cooperative spirit often lessens students' personal burdens and gives them more incentive to complete assignments. Again, planning the trip will be more fun and meaningful if the traveler sees the trip as feasible and necessary.

Student Issues

Nature of the Beast

Many students may be extremely opinionated about certain topics, due to family background, personal experiences, and peer group culture—or they may just be trying to assert themselves. Adolescents, in particular, are attempting to critically analyze the world about them. Many of the activities in *Lessons for Life* ask for students to investigate and share their personal belief systems. Tolerance of differences may be one of the greatest challenges of this curriculum, as well as one of its greatest accomplishments. It will be important to strike a balance between honoring individual opinions and keeping students from insulting and demeaning others with their opinions. All students need to be encouraged to listen and respect opinions, and respond to opposition with facts rather than personal attacks.

Motivation—Group and Individual

Motivation is foundational to getting students to seriously attend to the career development curriculum. If most members of a classroom are enthusiastic about a lesson, the rest usually will fall in line. Certain individuals within the classroom may also be instrumental in motivating classmates to consider the seriousness of a lesson. Knowing *who* and *what* motivate students will help you focus your energy on *how* to get students invested in their life development in substantive ways.

On an individual basis, what "turns on" one student may "turn off" another. Explaining this fact (and getting students to accept it) often allows students to feel they can share more freely—sometimes even in a negative fashion—and to sort out what motivates them.

Developmental Challenges

Chronological age or grade level never determines a student's developmental maturity. A lesson that seems appropriate for the majority of a class may "miss the mark" with a student who is still struggling with developmental issues that others have already mastered. Patience and understanding must be modeled by adults and nurtured in peers, as students who seem less mature or developmentally unready for some lessons struggle to make sense of their world. Referring back to previous lessons in a section of the book may give hints about topics or issues that a student may need to consider before a current lesson can make sense.

Individual Idiosyncrasies

There will be times when students may resist certain activities, such as role playing, because of self-consciousness or shyness. Describing the format of the activity and encouraging volunteers often eliminates lack of participation. When the whole class balks at an activity, present the objectives and ask them to create an alternative activity that will produce the same results.

Information That Can Be Shared with Others

It should be determined in advance that information shared in a portfolio and in class is not confidential. Students should be encouraged to talk with their teachers and counselors in advance of sharing any personal information that may make others uncomfortable. Should personal insights or issues be shared unexpectedly in class, the lesson facilitator should process the information prior to the end of class. Sometimes all that is needed is a gentle reminder about honoring a person's privacy and dignity. "Teachable moments" such as these can contribute to the developmental and maturational life of students at any age—if handled with respect and sensitivity.

Confidentiality

There may be times when students disclose information in their portfolios or in small-group discussions that truly should remain confidential. For example, in the Personal Notes box in the Self-Knowledge section of the *Get a Life* portfolio, occasionally a student might make a statement about suicide or abuse issues. Obviously, such a student is asking for help. The school counselor should be involved and the student should be encouraged to share the concern—but not in the portfolio. If a school does not have a clear policy about confidentiality, then such a policy should become a priority and faculty and staff should be apprised of their responsibilities or obligations.

Special Needs

It is extremely important to take into consideration students' special needs (e.g., auditory processing problems, eye–hand coordination difficulties, writing deficits, etc.). Modification of activities should be made with little disruption to the class and the activity. Students with special needs should be reassured that modifications are considered an essential part of learning.

Individual Planning and Advising

A great deal of personal growth can be attained through group activities; however, some individual contact with a teacher or counselor may be essential for personal, academic, or career planning. Students should be aware of procedures for seeing an advisor for an appointment. Essentially, all the lessons in this book are designed to facilitate individual planning and advising. Individuals need to plan their own lives, but they usually need some advice along the way. It's important to have receptive adults who can appreciate students' individual journeys while lending support when needed.

Summary

Entire college courses are devoted to some of the topics we have discussed in this chapter. We recognize that a single chapter cannot do justice to the importance of the management issues, classroom issues, and student issues that can confound and compound the delivery of a school's curriculum. However, in highlighting some of these important issues, it is our hope that we can both create an appreciation for the "big picture" that complements curriculum implementation and at the same time provide some useful advice that will make the delivery of these lessons more plausible and enjoyable.

A high-quality developmental career guidance curriculum requires quality management, quality content, and quality instruction. The astute educator will recognize the areas in this chapter that require further study and development, and seek the resources to enhance the knowledge and skills that will assure successful fulfillment of the program goals. Plan the trip accordingly.

And now, let us introduce the *Lessons for Life …*

Chapter Four

In the Driver's Seat

Lessons to Promote Self-Knowledge

We need to be in the driver's seat when it comes to exploring career options and making important life decisions. Having other people make our career decisions for us is like having a chauffeur—or even worse, a designated driver! If we hand over the wheel to others, we are either admitting that we don't want to be responsible for the ride or we may feel our own driving abilities are impaired. This is one ride where we can't afford the luxury of letting someone else take the wheel; therefore, we have to assume responsibility and make sure nothing is impairing our ability to enjoy the ride.

When you settle into that driver's seat, only you know what makes you comfortable: Is there enough head room? Is there lumbar support? Can your feet reach the pedals? Does the rearview mirror allow you to see where you've been? Is your seatbelt fastened? Do you have a good grip on the wheel? Is it the kind of vehicle you really enjoy driving? Self-knowledge is the key to feeling confident about and comfortable with the career journey you are about to embark upon. Self-knowledge is critical before any movement of the vehicle is initiated.

Good career choices rely on finding a good "fit" between the individual and the occupation. A comfortable fit in career decision making first of all requires an awareness of what makes the individual unique. Do you prefer working with data, people, things, or ideas? Would you rather work indoors or outdoors? What do you find fascinating? What bores you? What rewards do you seek from work? How important is work related to other things in your life? Recognizing who you are helps give you a clear, "bug-free" windshield. Self-knowledge helps you sit comfortably in the driver's seat and assures you of having a dashboard free of obstacles that could distract you or interfere with your attention to the road. Self-confidence puts you in the driver's seat. Although passengers or backseat drivers may have opinions or input about which direction you should take or what they think of your driving habits, you are still the one who needs to make the important decisions behind the wheel. Of course, recognizing that those influences can sometimes shift you into forward or reverse is understanding what growth is all about. Being receptive to wise advice may promote changes for the better—and perhaps provide for a smoother and more scenic adventure.

Essentially, self-knowledge provides students with the operator's license to get on the road, and to appreciate the journey. When they begin to define themselves, they can more appropriately interact with peers and adults who can caution and enlighten them about the career process. Self-knowledge is the power that fuels the vehicle of change and growth. Along the journey, total empowerment will rely on regular refueling and maintenance.

This chapter includes lesson plans and activities for helping students find the fuel to start and maintain their career journeys. Five different components of Self-Knowledge are addressed: Self-Concept, Interpersonal Skills, Growth and Change, Employability Skills, and Decision Making. Three different lessons are provided for each component, and a number of reproducible worksheets are included for student reinforcement of the lessons. The key to using this self-knowledge is in integrating it in such a way that students can't wait to turn on the ignition and get started.

I'M SOMETHING SPECIAL
Self-Knowledge
"Self-Concept"

OBJECTIVES:

1. Students will be able to share ways in which they are special.

2. Students will identify ways that fingerprints are unique to each individual.

3. Students will explore the process of discovering individual talents and strengths.

SUPPLIES:

Something Special by David McPhail, Boston: Little, Brown & Company, 1988. Surrounded by parents and siblings with remarkable talents, Sam yearns to be good at something and finds his own special niche when he discovers the pleasure of painting.

Large paper egg cut out for each student

Water-color tray paints

Basket filled with artificial grass

PORTFOLIO ENTRY: *Self-Knowledge,* Self-Concept, *"Strengths" or "Personal Qualities"*

I'M SOMETHING SPECIAL!
Self-Knowledge
"Self-Concept"

LESSON	NOTES
1. **Introduction:** Tell students that people are special in their own ways. This story talks about someone who has difficulty finding out how he is special. Read *Something Special*. Briefly discuss the story and review the individual characters and their talents that make them special.	
2. **Focus:** Share the fact that each person is special for many reasons. One thing that we all have that is special is our fingerprints.	
3. **Activity:** Each student receives a paper egg, either plain or with a facial expression, to decorate with his/her fingerprints using dampened water-color paints (put student's name on the back of egg). While the students uniquely decorate the eggs, have them think of one way that they are special. When finished, have students share the ways they are special and place decorated eggs in a basket as a classroom decoration.	
4. **Closure:** Ask: What did we do in this lesson? What did we learn about ourselves? What did we learn about others? Why is this basket so special?	

EGG FACES

EGG PATTERNS

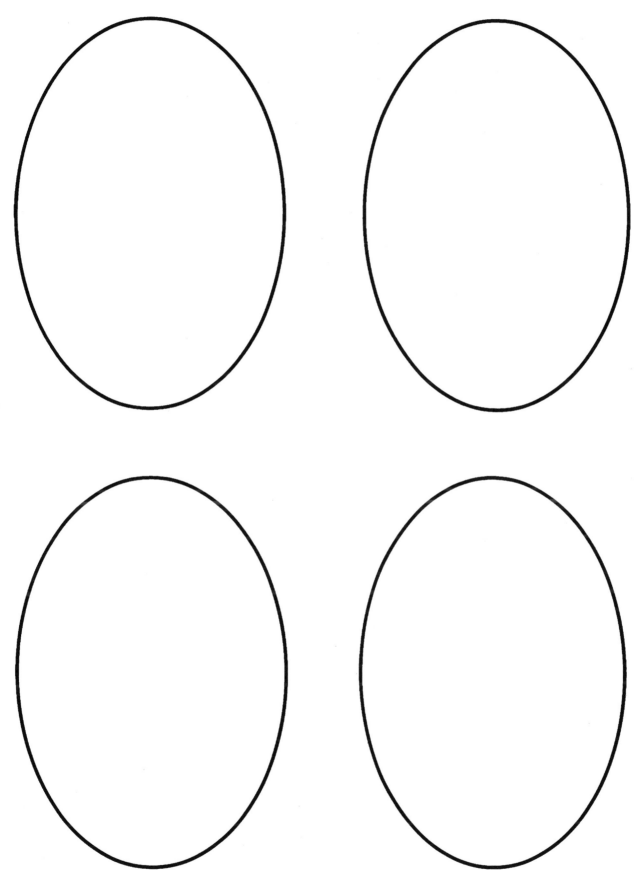

FLYING HIGH
Self-Knowledge
"Self-Concept"

OBJECTIVES:

1. Students will be able to share experiences that make them naturally exhilarated.

2. Students will be able to label accomplishments that make them feel good about themselves.

3. Students will be able to identify their accomplishments in drawing or writing.

SUPPLIES:

Large kite-shaped paper (pattern provided)

3-inch paper circles (pattern provided)

Glue stick

PORTFOLIO ENTRY: *My Personal Career Plan*, Self-Knowledge, *"Unique Self"* or *"Personal Qualities"*

FLYING HIGH!
Self-Knowledge
"Self-Concept"

LESSON	NOTES
1. **Introduction:** Ask students how many have ever flown a kite. Ask how it is done. Have students explain the difficult and easy parts. Ask how it feels when you've worked a long time to fly the kite and you've finally accomplished it.	
2. **Focus:** Have students think about other personal accomplishments that make them feel good about themselves. Have students think about activities that are done alone, with family, and with friends and ask for an example of each.	
3. **Activity:** Have students draw or write in a 3" colored circle about a time when they felt good about something they did alone, with family, or with friends (10 min.). Share those times with the group and glue the circles on the kite as a decoration. Display the kites in your classroom.	
4. **Closure:** Review the lesson. Ask students: What did you learn about yourself? What did you learn about your classmates? Why is the kite important? What did you like best about this lesson? Did you dislike anything about this lesson? Will you share this with your family?	

KITE PATTERN

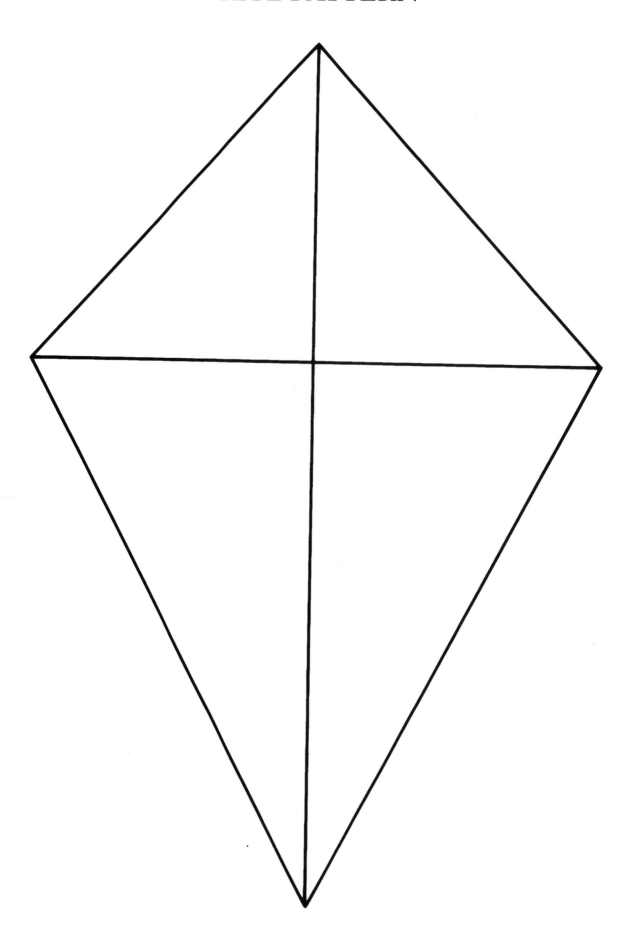

CIRCLE PATTERNS

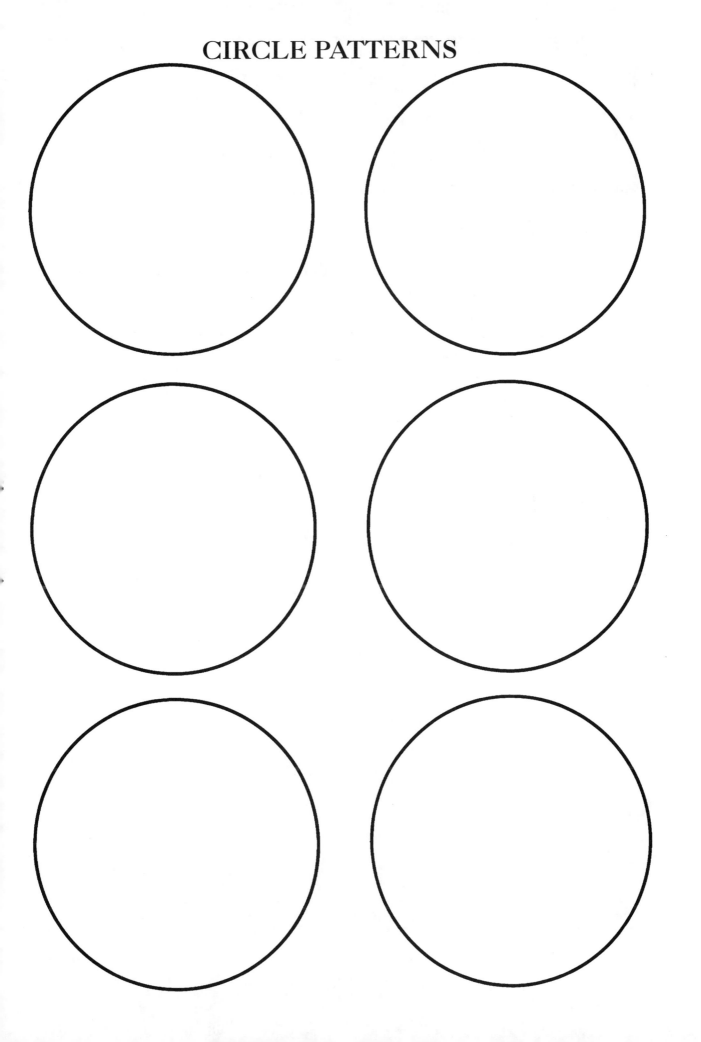

NAME THAT KID
Self-Knowledge
"Self-Concept"

OBJECTIVES:

1. Students will be able to identify positive attributes of classmates.

2. Students will be able to develop complimentary clues about classmates based on looks and actions.

3. Students will be able to discuss their feelings about compliments.

SUPPLIES:

Bongo drum or tambourine

PORTFOLIO ENTRY: *Self-Knowledge,* Interpersonal Skills, *"Things Friends Like"*

NAME THAT KID
Self-Knowledge
"Self-Concept"

LESSON	NOTES
1. **Introduction:** Demonstrate different rhythms that can be made on a tambourine or bongo. Ask students to create an original rhythm, then share a time when they felt important. Have students share individually.	
2. **Focus:** Explain that people feel important when someone notices them. We notice people by the way they look and the way they act. Have students give some examples of each. Encourage students to give clues that show positive academic and social traits of classmates.	
3. **Activity:** Explain that they will be playing "Name That Kid," a game that uses clues about looks and actions to describe a classmate. A student will give 3 clues about a classmate, using 1 clue about looks and 2 clues about actions. Students may guess once after each clue. The winner gets the next turn. If the class is stumped, the clue-giver gives the answer and chooses the next person.	
4. **Closure:** Ask: How did you like the game? What made it fun? What were the hard parts? Easy parts? How did it make you feel? What did you learn?	

COMPLIMENT WEB
Self-Knowledge
"Interpersonal Skills"

OBJECTIVES:

1. Students will be able to identify positive attributes of classmates.

2. Students will be able to verbalize compliments to classmates based on looks and actions.

3. Students will be able to discuss their feelings about compliments.

SUPPLIES:

Large circular piece of paper approximately 4′ in diameter with students' names spaced evenly around the border

Large marker

VARIATION:

Decide how many student names to put on the circle. You may want to cluster certain groups of students together, depending on group needs.

PORTFOLIO ENTRY: *Self-Knowledge,* Interpersonal Skills, *"I Look for Friends"*

COMPLIMENT WEB
Self-Knowledge
"Interpersonal Skills"

LESSON	NOTES
1. **Introduction:** Ask students to share a time when they felt important.	
2. **Focus:** Explain that people feel important when other people notice the way they look and the way they act. Have students give examples of each. Encourage students to give positive social and academic traits of classmates.	
3. **Activity:** Students will gather around a circular paper near their names. They will be asked to give a compliment to a classmate based on looks or actions. After the compliment is given, they draw a line with the marker from their name to the complimented person. That person will thank the giver and proceed to compliment another classmate. The process continues until everyone has been complimented. The result is a web of the compliments.	
4. **Closure:** Tell students that compliments affect the receiver and others, just as if one thread of a web were plucked, it would affect the other threads. Ask: How does it feel to receive a compliment? How does it feel to give a compliment? Why is it important to give compliments? What happens to a group when you give compliments?	

OBJECTIVES:

1. Students will be able to give positive compliments to classmates.

2. Students will be able to identify ways that positive and negative comments have an effect on group participation.

3. Students will be able to discuss their individual influence on group participation.

SUPPLIES:

Chart paper

Markers

PORTFOLIO ENTRY: *Self-Knowledge,* Interpersonal Skills, Competency Skills, *"Greatest Challenge" or "Ways to Influence"*

MAKE 'EM SHINE
Self-Knowledge
"Interpersonal Skills"

LESSON	NOTES
1. **Introduction:** Give examples of compliments based on looks and actions. Then have students give examples of each.	
2. **Focus:** Have students form two lines facing each other to form a human car wash. Students are the sprayers, washers, dryers, and waxers (a few on each side). One student or the teacher slowly walks down the middle and receives compliments from each student to shine them up—just like a car wash. This activity can be used on a special occasion or whenever someone is having a bad day and needs a "shine."	
3. **Activity:** In a large or small group discussion, have students brainstorm comments that encourage group participation, and those that discourage group participation. Label them turn-ons and turn-offs and chart responses.	
4. **Closure:** Ask: What did you learn about compliments and groups? What did you learn about turn-ons and turn-offs? Can you think of times when you can help a group by giving a turn-on? Why is it important to know this? Practice this in class.	

OBJECTIVES:

1. Students will be able to identify the feelings of being left out after playing a game.

2. Students will be able to discuss the importance of including classmates in activities.

3. Students will be able to identify methods of including classmates into group activities.

SUPPLIES:

Chart paper

Markers

PORTFOLIO ENTRY: *Self-Knowledge,* Interpersonal Skills, *"Role Models"*

MINGLE AND GROUP
Self-Knowledge
"Interpersonal Skills"

LESSON	NOTES

1. **Introduction:** Tell students that they will work quietly and individually in a designated area. The teacher will give a command to "Group in __." (Provide a number, such as threes, fours, etc.) As students hustle into groups, some students inevitably will be "left out." Ask those students to remember how they felt to be left out.

   Continue giving commands to the students using different numbers until only two students are left out. Then tell the "left outs" that they are the winners (so all "lefts outs" feel like winners).

2. **Focus:** Ask students to share their feelings about the game. How did they feel when they were left out? How did the last players feel at first? How did they feel as "left out"? How did the group feel as winners?

3. **Activity:** Ask students why it is important to include classmates into a group. Why do people leave others out? How do others feel? How do they feel? List suggestions that help students include classmates in activities.

4. **Closure:** Ask: What did you learn about being left out? Why is it important to include others in activities? How can you include others at home? At school? Can you try one suggestion this week?

CHANGE VS. SAME
Self-Knowledge
"Growth and Change"

OBJECTIVES:

1. Students will be able to recognize change in themselves.

2. Students will be able to recognize consistency in themselves and others.

3. Students will be able to recognize that with change in age comes change in responsibility.

SUPPLIES:

Love You Forever by Robert Munsche, Willowdale, Ontario: Firefly Books Ltd., 1986. This is the story of how a little boy goes through the stages of childhood and becomes a man. It is also the story of the enduring nature of parents' love.

PORTFOLIO ENTRY: *Self-Knowledge,* Growth and Development, *"Concerns"*

CHANGE VS. SAME
Self-Knowledge
"Growth and Change"

LESSON	NOTES
1. **Introduction:** Tell students that the lesson will focus on how things change and how things stay the same.	
2. **Focus:** Ask students how they have changed since they were babies (e.g., height, weight, etc.). Ask how they have stayed the same (e.g., color of eyes, color of hair, etc.).	
3. **Activity:** Read the story *Love You Forever.*	
4. **Closure:** Ask students what things changed in the story. What things stayed the same? How did the child's responsibility change? What did you learn about change? What did you learn about responsibility and change?	

BLOOMING
Self-Knowledge
"Growth and Change"

OBJECTIVES:

1. Students will be able to recognize skills they can accomplish.

2. Students will be able to recognize that gaining new skills requires time, interest, and growth.

3. Students will be able to describe future skills they hope to attain.

SUPPLIES:

Leo the Late Bloomer by Robert Kraus, New York: Scholastic Book Services, 1971. A young tiger matures slowly. While his father worries and his mother nurtures, Leo blooms in his own time.

"Can Do" can worksheets for each student

Chart paper

Tape

PORTFOLIO ENTRY: *Self-Knowledge,* Growth and Development, *"Things I've Learned" or "Personal Skills"*

BLOOMING
Self-Knowledge
"Growth and Change"

LESSON	NOTES
1. **Introduction:** Tell students that they are changing every day. Ask them to share examples of things they can do in school that they couldn't do last year (e.g., reading, writing). As students share, have them write examples on the "Can Do" can. Then tape the cans on chart paper as if they are on shelves.	
2. **Focus:** Tell students that learning new skills takes time and practice. Ask them to recall the steps it took to learn a new skill (e.g., learning the alphabet, eating with a fork, etc.)	
3. **Activity:** Read *Leo the Late Bloomer.*	
4. **Closure:** Ask students what Leo's problem was. How did his parents feel? How did he feel? Did you ever feel this way? What did you learn from this story? Name one thing you'd like to learn when you are older. What will you need to do to acquire this skill? (Relate how adults learn skills to do jobs.)	

Shayna

Can Do

A, B, C, count 1-100, tie shoes, color inside the lines, sing the school song

CRYSTAL BALL
Self-Knowledge
"Growth and Change"

OBJECTIVES:

1. Students will be able to project change in themselves over time.

2. Students will be able to identify activities accomplishable in 5, 10, and 20 years.

3. Students will be able to recognize similar goals among peers for the future.

SUPPLIES:

"Crystal Ball" worksheet for each student

PORTFOLIO ENTRY: *Self-Knowledge,* Growth and Development, *"Concerns about Future"* or *"Improve Self"*

CRYSTAL BALL
Self-Knowledge
"Growth and Change"

LESSON	NOTES
1. **Introduction:** Tell students that they will have an opportunity to look into the future and predict what their lives might be like.	
2. **Focus:** Determine the approximate age of the students in 5, 10, and 20 years.	
3. **Activity:** Pass out crystal ball worksheets. Ask each student to write or draw one activity in each category. Allow 20 minutes. Offer assistance to students who have difficulty. Ask students to share their crystal ball activities.	
4. **Closure:** Ask: What did you learn about yourself? What did you learn about your classmates? Why did we do this lesson? Why is it important?	

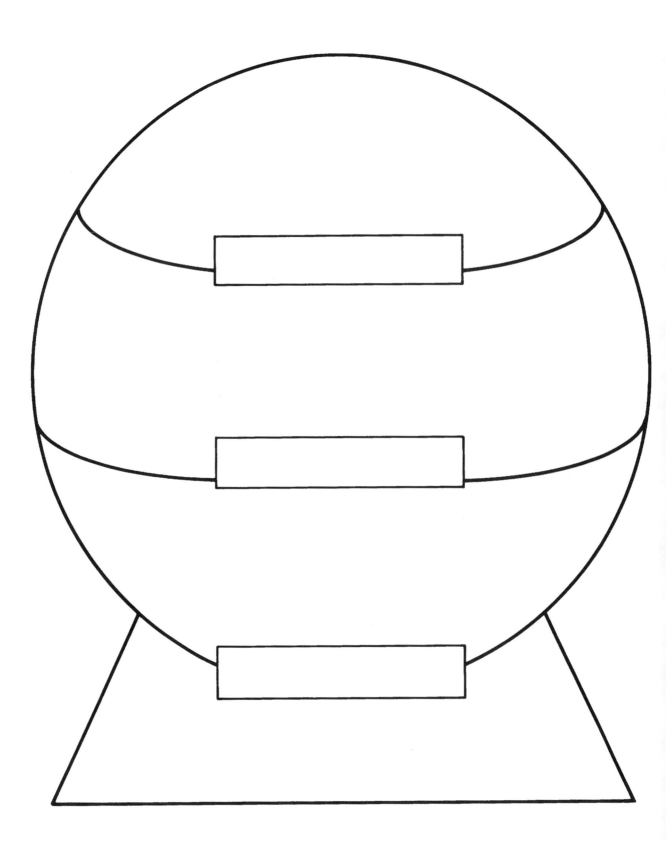

Sample student worksheet

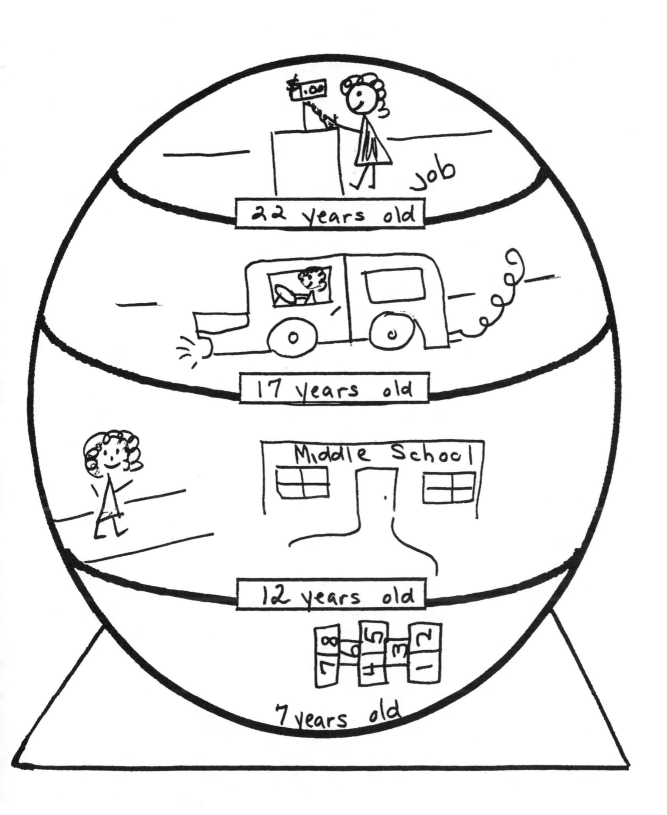

OBJECTIVES:

1. Students will be able to share personal experiences when they were worried or upset about a situation.

2. Students will be able to identify a worrisome situation and possible solutions.

3. Students will be able to apply the steps in Objective 2 to life situations.

SUPPLIES:

Chart paper

Markers

WHY WORRY?
Self-Knowledge
"Employability Skills"

LESSON	NOTES
1. **Introduction:** Ask students to share a time when they were worried or upset about a situation. Give an example, including both home and school situations. List the students' situations on chart paper.	
2. **Focus:** Explain that worrying is an activity that doesn't help a situation. Worrying only wastes time and energy. Tell students that it is much more helpful to DO something when they are able. Doing something about the situation will help them feel better. If nothing can be done, they need to find activities that will take their minds off the situation.	
3. **Activity:** Choose a situation from the chart list. Have a student identify the problem clearly and suggest possible solutions. Ask the individual student who shared the problem to choose and try the best solution. (Follow up in later classes to evaluate the choice.) Continue through the list, as time allows, remembering also to choose ones that are out of students' immediate control, e.g., the weather or a terminal illness.	
4. **Closure:** Ask: What did we talk about today? Why is it important to know what to do when we are worried? When can you use this information? What did you like/dislike about this lesson? Share your ideas with other adults.	

WHATZYER PROBLEM?
Self-Knowledge
"Employability Skills"

OBJECTIVES:

1. Students will be able to share personal experiences about the decisions they already made that day.

2. Students will be able to identify the six steps in problem solving.

3. Students will be able to apply the six steps to a classroom problem in a large group setting.

SUPPLIES:

Chart paper

Markers

Problem-solving posters

PORTFOLIO ENTRY: *Self-Knowledge,* Personal Skills *or* Decision-Making Skills, *"Describe the Process"*

WHATZYER PROBLEM?
Self-Knowledge
"Employability Skills"

LESSON	NOTES

1. **Introduction:** Ask students to share examples of some of the decisions they had already made that day. Ask them to rate the decisions as difficult or easy to solve. Explain that some decisions are easy because we make them frequently and have had positive experiences when making them in the past. Difficult decisions are ones that we have never made before, or ones that we've made poor choices about in the past. There is a step-by-step procedure that will help the next time a difficult decision occurs.

2. **Focus:** Introduce the six steps in problem solving by charting them, or presenting them on posters, and discuss the importance of each in order:
   - Say the problem
   - Brainstorm all possible solutions
   - Consider the consequences
   - Choose
   - Act
   - Evaluate

3. **Activity:** Ask the teacher to suggest a class problem that might be solved using the six steps. Lead the students through the process and ask them to abide by the "teacher-approved" class decision. Set a date to evaluate the decision.

4. **Closure:** Ask: What did we do today? Why is it important to know how to problem solve? When will you be able to use these steps? Share these steps with adults.

OBJECTIVES:

1. Students will be able to discuss the responsibilities of specific jobs at a carnival.

2. Students will be able to privately choose a carnival job that best suits their personal positive characteristics.

3. Students will be able to discuss the positive attributes of their classmates and guess their carnival job choice.

SUPPLIES:

Chart paper

Markers

Small pieces of papers for each student

3-inch stars (pattern provided)

Poster board

PORTFOLIO ENTRY: *Self-Knowledge,* Interpersonal Skills, *"When Others Meet Me"*

CARNIVAL TIME
Self-Knowledge
"Employability Skills"

LESSON	NOTES
1. **Introduction:** Have students pretend that they are going to put on a carnival. The booths at the carnival will include: • selling food • darts and balloons • pony rides • talent show • games and races Write the names of the booths on chart paper.	
2. **Focus:** Have students discuss the responsibilities at each booth and discuss what personal attributes would contribute to the success of each booth. Chart answers on separate sheets.	
3. **Activity:** Have students privately write down their personal choice of a carnival job and their reasons why, based on their individual talents. Individually, have students guess the choices of classmates, describing the personal positive attribute that would contribute to the success of the booth. Chart the talents as they are mentioned. Have students select one of the positive attributes and write it along with his/her name in a star. When all have shared, review all the positive attributes that are in the class and make a poster with the stars entitled, "A Class Full of Stars."	
4. **Closure:** Ask: What did you learn about yourself? What did you learn about your classmates individually and as a group? Why is it important to recognize talents in others?	

Sample student "Stars"

Jan
organized

Kim
likes
children

Alex
Helpful

Chris
talented

Sam
knows
about
horses

STYLE SHOW
Self-Knowledge
"Decision Making"

OBJECTIVES:

1. Students will be able to divide themselves equally into small groups.

2. Students will be able to complete a small group project with all members participating and cooperating.

3. Students will be able to verbalize the cooperative skills used during the group project.

SUPPLIES:

Newspaper

Stapler

Staples

PORTFOLIO ENTRY: *Self-Knowledge,* Decision Making *or* Personal Skills, *"Describe the Process"*

STYLE SHOW
Self-Knowledge
"Decision Making"

LESSON	NOTES
1. **Introduction:** Tell students that they have the task of dividing themselves into two small groups with equal (if possible) numbers of boys and girls. Allow them to do this independently. When the two groups are formed, ask them to form a third group so that all are as equal as possible. Tell them a fun-filled activity will follow.	
2. **Focus:** Tell the groups that they will be creating a costume for one member of their group, after they agree on a model.	
3. **Activity:** Explain that they will have approximately 20 minutes to create a costume for their model using only newspapers and a stapler. Each member of the group, including the model, is expected to design a part of the costume. When time is up, each member of the group will point out his or her design. Should inappropriate group behavior occur, the teacher/adult may withdraw the stapler from the group until they can resolve their differences.	
4. **Closure:** Ask: What did you like or not like about this activity? What skills were necessary for the group to be successful? Give examples of appropriate group behavior.	

LET'S BAKE A CAKE
Self-Knowledge
"Decision Making"

OBJECTIVES:

1. Students will be able to verbalize the importance of making good decisions.

2. Students will be able to recognize the importance of prioritizing their decisions.

3. Students will be able to apply ordered decision making to life situations.

SUPPLIES:

Cake decorations

A strip of poster board for each direction

Answer sheet

VARIATION:

Students may individually organize the directions by cutting out each step in strips, organizing them, and gluing them to paper in order.

PORTFOLIO ENTRY: *Self-Knowledge,* Decision Making *or* Personal Skills, *"Problem Solving"*

LET'S BAKE A CAKE
Self-Knowledge
"Decision Making"

LESSON	NOTES

1. **Introduction:** Ask students why it is important to make good decisions. Why is it important to make some decisions before you make others?

2. **Focus:** Ask students why it is important to make decisions in the right order when making a cake.

3. **Activity:** Pass out cake directions in scrambled order to 13 students. Have the students line up as they are passed out. Read the scrambled directions. Ask for suggestions to improve the directions. Have students organize themselves into the step-by-step order of the recipe and discuss the importance.

4. **Closure:** What did you learn about decision making? Can you give examples of other situations when it is important to order your decision making?

5. **Follow-up:** Create a decision-making process for a "real-life" situation. Brainstorm the steps, then put on poster board and repeat the exercise.

LET'S BAKE A CAKE

Directions: Cut out each step. Put the steps for baking a cake in the correct order and present on paper.

PREHEAT OVEN TO 350°

COOL

BREAK 2 EGGS AND BEAT

BAKE FOR 35 MINUTES

GREASE A 9″ PAN

SIFT AND MEASURE FLOUR

CUT AND EAT

MELT BUTTER

POUR INTO CAKE PAN

MEASURE SUGAR

ADD SPICES

DECORATE WITH FROSTING

COMBINE EGGS, SUGAR, BUTTER, AND FLOUR

"LET'S BAKE A CAKE" ANSWER SHEET

Reprint the following when students have completed the activity so they can self-check their accuracy.

1   PREHEAT OVEN TO 350°

2   SIFT AND MEASURE FLOUR

3   MELT BUTTER

4   MEASURE SUGAR

5   BREAK 2 EGGS AND BEAT

6   COMBINE EGGS, SUGAR, BUTTER, AND FLOUR

7   ADD SPICES

8   GREASE A 9″ PAN

9   POUR INTO CAKE PAN

10   BAKE FOR 35 MINUTES

11   COOL

12   DECORATE WITH FROSTING

13   CUT AND EAT

TAKING STOCK OF YOUR OPTIONS
Self-Knowledge
"Decision Making"

OBJECTIVES:

1. Students will be able to identify decisions they will be making in the next five years.

2. Students will be able to identify the five most important decisions they will be making in the next five years.

3. Students will be able to prioritize the most important decisions in chronological and personal-choice order.

SUPPLIES:

None

PORTFOLIO ENTRY: *Self-Knowledge,* Decision Making or Personal Qualities, *"Describe the Process"*

TAKING STOCK OF YOUR OPTIONS
Self-Knowledge
"Decision Making"

LESSON	NOTES
1. **Introduction:** Ask students to think about being five years older. Have them discuss age, grade, school, etc.	
2. **Focus:** Ask students to give one example of a decision they will be making in the next five years. Tell them to brainstorm 15 other decisions they will be making. (This can be done individually, in pairs, or in small groups.)	
3. **Activity:** Share in a large group the brainstormed examples. Students may add to or change their lists. Ask them to check the five they are most excited about making. Have students list those five in chronological order. Discuss. Going back to their longer list, now have them re-order the decisions in order of personal choice.	
4. **Closure:** Ask: What was the purpose of this lesson? Why is it important?	

CHAPTER FIVE

Nice Set o' Wheels

Lessons to Help Students Examine Life Roles

Nothing makes for a smooth ride like a great set of tires. The tires and wheels create the support for the vehicle that will act as a buffer between the rough road and the car's occupants. The wheels are connected to the frame of the car, serving as the means for turning the car in various directions, and absorbing many of the bumps and stressors that seem to appear along the road. The wheels need to be properly aligned if the car is to respond well and stay on a steady course without veering too far to the left or right. The tires cover the wheels and help provide the proper traction both for creating a comfortable ride and for moving the vehicle through the slippery spots. To give this kind of ride, the tires need to be well balanced and have just the right amount of inflation. The quality of the ride is almost always seen in the quality of the tire.

A student's career journey deserves and requires a strong foundation—a support system that can help the student make the proper turns, weather the rough spots, and maintain a steady course. Students need to understand the impact of family, friends, and other influences in their lives that contribute to their beliefs, aspirations, and sense of meaningfulness. Just as the wheels need to be aligned and the tires balanced, students need to have a sense of the rules by which they operate and what creates balance in their lives. In exploring their life roles, some students will find it reaffirming to note the cultural and sociological influences on their development. For other students, this exploration may reveal imbalances that need to be corrected if they are to avoid a rough journey. Of course, when it comes to inflation, we want students to surround themselves with a support system that helps them build a healthy self-esteem without becoming overly inflated. Some of that inflation can come from others, but a significant amount of the pressure needs to come from within, as students internalize the important messages and guidelines that shape their decision making and goal setting. Remember, a minimal amount of pressure and an adequate amount of inflation are good things. Students need to have a sense of where that good pressure and good inflation come from. They also need to know how to use that knowledge to create balance in their lives and to support them on their career journey.

In this chapter, five different components of one's Life Roles are explored: Cultural Heritage, Understanding Roles, Acceptance of Others, Assertiveness Skills, and the Use of Leisure Time. The three lessons under each component allow students to explore their own life roles, while they also nurture tolerance and acceptance of others' life roles. A number of reproducible student worksheets are included for reinforcement of the lessons. This set of lessons is particularly helpful for including families in the career exploration process.

Because students may be introduced to new words and concepts about life roles (e.g., rituals, heritage, roles, occupations, etc.), you may want to infuse a vocabulary list as a complement to these lessons. Students will be able to see how their vocabulary development relates to their career and personal development.

Once again, the challenge for educators is to help students reflect on these lessons and find ways to integrate their insights within the career awareness-exploration-preparation framework.

FAMILY PORTRAITS
Life Roles
"Cultural Heritage"

OBJECTIVES:

1. Students will be able to draw pictures of their families doing an activity together.

2. Students will be able to share their pictures in a large group setting.

3. Students will be able to recognize and appreciate the differences in family structure and activities.

SUPPLIES:

Large drawing paper

Markers

Crayons

FAMILY PORTRAITS
Life Roles
"Cultural Heritage"

LESSON	NOTES
1. **Introduction:** Tell students that the topic of the lesson will be the family. Discuss their meaning of family.	
2. **Focus:** Brainstorm with students family activities that are enjoyed by each member.	
3. **Activity:** Ask students to draw pictures of their individual families doing an activity together. Encourage students to include all people who they consider part of their family. Some students may wish to divide their papers in half to include parents not living with them. Allow 20 minutes. Have students share their pictures in a large group setting and after every fourth or fifth sharing, compare and contrast family sizes, make-up, and activities.	
4. **Closure:** Ask: How many of you would enjoy the activities of other families? Share which ones interest you. Why are families different? Why are families important? What can we learn from this lesson?	

WHAT'S IN A NAME?
Life Roles
"Cultural Heritage"

OBJECTIVES:

1. Students will be able to investigate their families' ethnic backgrounds.

2. Students will be able to chart the ethnic backgrounds of their classmates.

3. Students will be able to share ethnic recipes that are part of their families' heritage.

SUPPLIES:

Parent note (provided)

2-inch colored paper squares (pattern provided)

Chart paper

PORTFOLIO ENTRY: *Life Roles,* Family Influence, *"Family Feels Important" or "Learned about Others"*

WHAT'S IN A NAME?
Life Roles
"Cultural Heritage"

LESSON	NOTES
1. **Introduction:** Share a personal story of your ancestry, mentioning the countries that are represented in your heritage. Explain how people in your family came to your country for various reasons.	
2. **Focus:** Explain to students that they will be creating a bar graph that illustrates the ethnic mix of the class. Discuss the importance of appreciating the cultural and ethnic contributions that are part of the class community. Have students investigate their heritage with their parents (note to parents attached).	
3. **Activity:** In small groups, have students list all the nationalities represented. In large group, have students share their findings, while the teacher charts the nationality horizontally on chart paper. (Chart each nationality only once, e.g., Greek, Native American.) Pass out one colored paper square for each nationality represented in a student's heritage. As students share, have them place a square over the mentioned nationality to form a bar graph.	
4. **Closure:** Ask: What did we create in this lesson? What did we discover? How did you go about finding your heritage? Is it important?	
5. **Follow-up:** Ask students if they eat food that represents their heritage. Ask students to bring in their favorite ethnic family recipe. These may be compiled and reproduced for all students in the class.	
6. **Enrichment:** Have students cook and share with their classmates the recipe they contributed to the cookbook.	

Dear Parents,

This week the students in our class will be discussing their families' ethnic backgrounds. They will be given a brief introduction in class and then asked to solicit your help in investigating the nationalities represented in your family heritage. Realizing that many nationalities may be represented, we would ask that students bring into class no more than the four major nationalities represented in their heritage lines.

Our activities highlight the wonderful lessons that can be learned from one's family. Please take this opportunity to share stories about your nationality, customs, and typical foods enjoyed by your family that reflect your ancestry.

A follow-up assignment will include sharing a recipe for a favorite ethnic food. A compilation of these recipes will result in a class cookbook. Eventually, if parents and students agree, we will celebrate its publication with an international banquet and taste-testing party. I hope that this unit will enrich the lives of your children and make them more aware of the ethnic diversity of their classmates.

Thank you for your active participation in the education of your child.

Sincerely,

RITUALS
Life Roles
"Cultural Heritage"

OBJECTIVES:

1. Students will be able to define the term "ritual" and understand how the practice of rituals reflects cultural heritage in families.

2. Students will be able to personalize family rituals by sharing photographs of their families.

3. Students will be able to appreciate and show respect for the cultural heritage of their classmates.

SUPPLIES:

Dictionary

Photographs of students depicting family rituals

PORTFOLIO ENTRY: *Life Roles,* Acceptance of Self and Others, *"Cultural Heritage" or "Learned about Others"*

RITUALS
Life Roles
"Cultural Heritage"

LESSON	NOTES
1. **Introduction:** Ask students to define the term "ritual." Discuss how family rituals reflect cultural heritage.	
2. **Focus:** Brainstorm rituals that families typically celebrate (e.g., births, deaths, religious ceremonies/holidays, weddings, rites of passage). Have students bring in up to five photographs that depict such rituals.	
3. **Activity:** In small groups, have individual students show their pictures and have the group guess which ritual is being celebrated. Encourage students to ask questions about rituals that they may not understand.	
4. **Closure:** In large group, ask: What did you learn about rituals? Why do families celebrate rituals differently? Give an example of a ritual that you would like to celebrate. Why is this lesson important? What can we do to show respect for different family rituals?	

ROLE CALL
Life Roles
"Understanding Roles"

OBJECTIVES:

1. Students will be able to recognize the varying roles that one person can hold simultaneously.

2. Students will be able to enumerate the roles that are assigned to themselves.

3. Students will be able to express their favorite role through art.

SUPPLIES:

Chart paper

Markers

Art paper

Crayons

PORTFOLIO ENTRY: *Life Roles,* Balance, *"Explores Own Life Roles"*

ROLE CALL
Life Roles
"Understanding Roles"

LESSON	NOTES
1. **Introduction:** Tell students that this lesson will show them how many "action" verbs that are made into nouns by adding an "er" to the end, often describe who they really are.	
2. **Focus:** Give students examples of "action" words that describe them (e.g., listener, singer, sister, brother, giver, babysitter, etc.). After listing and charting at least 25, ask students to choose ones from the list that describe them. Then have them continue to add examples to the list.	
3. **Activity:** Ask students to draw pictures of themselves in their favorite role. Tell them to think as they draw why this is their favorite role. Allow 20 minutes. In small groups, have students share their pictures and tell why they chose their roles.	
4. **Closure:** Ask: What did you learn about roles? Do parents and siblings have roles? Can you do more than one role at the same time? Do some roles conflict with each other? What roles make you a good student? worker? listener?	

GET THE PICTURE
Life Roles
"Understanding Roles"

OBJECTIVES:

1. Students will be able to recognize typical occupations in society.

2. Students will be able to recognize that gender bias exists in the workplace.

3. Students will be able to create collages that depict individuals performing nontraditional occupational tasks.

SUPPLIES:

Magazines

Art paper

Glue

PORTFOLIO ENTRY: *Life Roles, Understanding Roles, "Sex Role Stereotyping"*

GET THE PICTURE
Life Roles
"Understanding Roles"

LESSON	NOTES
1. **Introduction:** Show students a list of typical occupations in their communities (e.g., grocer, banker, firefighter, child care provider). Ask them to add to the list and briefly describe the tasks performed by each.	
2. **Focus:** Ask students to pick 10 occupations from the list and give a first name to a person who might hold such a job (e.g., Chris—the cook). In a large group, have students share their names and chart next to the occupation whether the name is male (M) or female (F). Ask students what the names are telling them. Discuss whether the duties required by the occupations must be performed by a certain gender.	
3. **Activity:** Have students create a collage of individuals performing nontraditional occupational tasks. Encourage creativity. Students may have to draw new faces on magazine cut-outs, or switch heads of pictures. Display collages in an area for others to see, and entitle the bulletin board, "Get the Picture: Understanding Roles."	
4. **Closure:** Ask: What did you learn from this activity? Is there a nontraditional occupation that might interest you? Do you know people who are in nontraditional occupations? What do you have to do in order for others to appreciate nontraditional job roles?	
5. **Follow-up:** Invite guest speakers to the class who have nontraditional occupations.	

BALANCING ACT
Life Roles
"Understanding Roles"

OBJECTIVES:

1. Students will be able to perform a cooperative group activity.

2. Students will be able to identify the roles necessary to accomplish the group tasks.

3. Students will be able to describe the importance of cooperative group roles in other settings.

SUPPLIES:

Masking tape

Carpet or floor area that has a space marked off by masking tape, approximately 7 feet by 7 feet, or enough room for all students to fit. Additional tape may be used to reduce the space to challenge second and third attempts.

PORTFOLIO ENTRY: *Life Roles,* Acceptance of Others, *"Things I've Learned"*

BALANCING ACT
Life Roles
"Understanding Roles"

LESSON	NOTES
1. **Introduction:** Tell students that the lesson will attempt to make them think about cooperation and the roles individuals play when they are cooperating.	
2. **Focus:** Tell students that you will ask them to assemble themselves in a space marked off by tape. Before they begin, ask them to enumerate the varying roles that individuals will need to assume in order to successfully complete the task.	
3. **Activity:** Give students about five minutes to discuss how they will approach the task. Tell them that once the activity begins, they will not be able to talk. If the silence is broken, the activity will begin again without a group conference. (Timing the activity is optional, but it adds an additional challenge.) If the task should be accomplished easily, suggest that they challenge themselves to less time or space.	
4. **Closure:** Ask: What was the purpose of this lesson? Why was it important to identify roles that would be played in the activity? Who played those roles successfully? What other group settings have roles—either assigned or assumed? Who is assigned and who assumes?	
5. **Follow-up:** Create other group physical challenges and repeat the same exercise.	

FAVORITE THINGS
Life Roles
"Acceptance of Others"

OBJECTIVES:

1. Students will be able to express and show their uniqueness through rhythm on a percussion instrument.

2. Students will be able to share their favorite things.

3. Students will be able to compare and contrast their favorite things with those of their classmates.

SUPPLIES:

Bongo drum or tambourine

"Favorite Things" worksheet

Pencils

FAVORITE THINGS
Life Roles
"Acceptance of Others"

LESSON	NOTES

1. **Introduction:** Show students how to play the bongo or tambourine. Demonstrate different ways to play them, and unique rhythms that can be made. In a round robin, have students say their names and create an original rhythm on the instrument to show that they are unique and special.

2. **Focus:** Explain to students that it is important for them to know and accept themselves before they can get to know and accept others. One way they get to know themselves is by determining what they like.

3. **Activity:** Have students return to seats and fill out "Favorite Things" worksheet individually, and star two that they would like to share with the class. (This sheet can be expanded for older students.) When completed, have students share with the class. Point out the similarities and differences in their responses.

4. **Closure:** Why do you think we did this lesson? What did you learn about yourself? What did you learn about your classmates? What did you already know? Why is it important to share your likes? How does knowing what you like and sharing it with your classmates make you feel? What did you like about this lesson? What did you dislike about this lesson?

FAVORITE THINGS

Color: _____

Song: _____

Animal: _____

Game: _____

Name: _____

My name is: _____

FAVORITE THINGS

Color: Blue

Song: You are my Sunshine

Animal: Kangroo

Game: Uno

Name: Bo

My name is: Sam

OBJECTIVES:

1. Students will be able to work in a cooperative group to create a finished product.

2. Students will be able to identify the skills needed to accomplish each individual task in the cooperative project.

3. Students will be able to appreciate the need for understanding and appreciation of individual skills in a cooperative group setting.

SUPPLIES:

"Butterfly" for each group (pattern provided)

PORTFOLIO ENTRY: *Life Roles,* Career Connection, *"Reflections"*

BUTTERFLIES
Life Roles
"Acceptance of Others"

LESSON	NOTES

1. **Introduction:** Tell students that the lesson will be one that requires cooperation. Divide students into small groups of four or five.

2. **Focus:** Each group will need to decide on individuals who can accomplish the following tasks: tracing, cutting, coloring, gluing, checking and passing-it-in. Discuss the skills needed to accomplish each task.

3. **Activity:** Tell students that each group must create a butterfly by following these directions:

   - **Tracer:** traces all butterfly pieces

   - **Cutter:** cuts out all butterfly pieces

   - **Colorer:** colors all butterfly pieces

   - **Gluer:** Glues butterfly pieces in proper places

   - **Overseer:** Checks that all tasks have been done; passes the completed project into the teacher.

   Allow 20 minutes for the project.

4. **Closure:** Ask: What did you learn about depending on others? What did you learn in this lesson about cooperation? What did you like about this lesson? What did you dislike about this lesson? How can you practice cooperation in other situations?

BUTTERFLY PATTERN
(REPRODUCE ON CARDBOARD.)

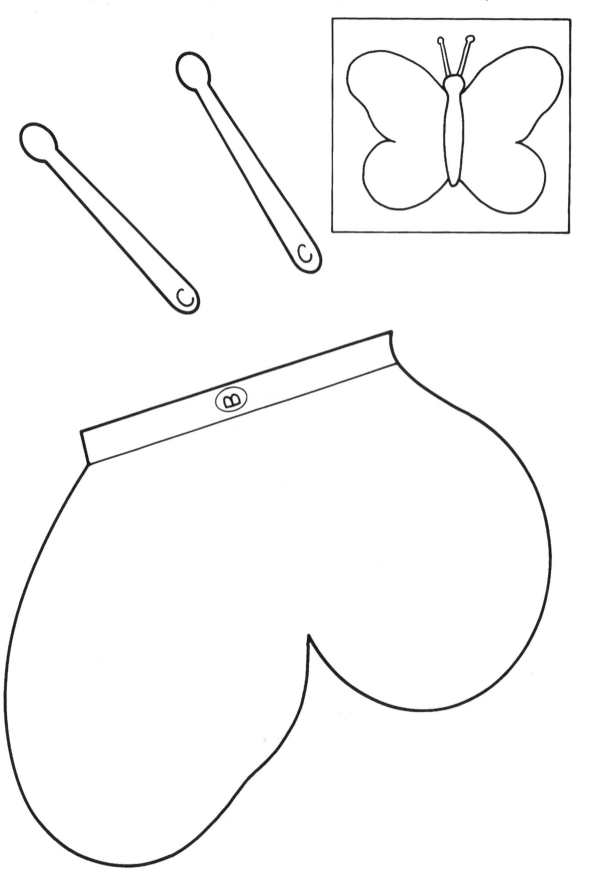

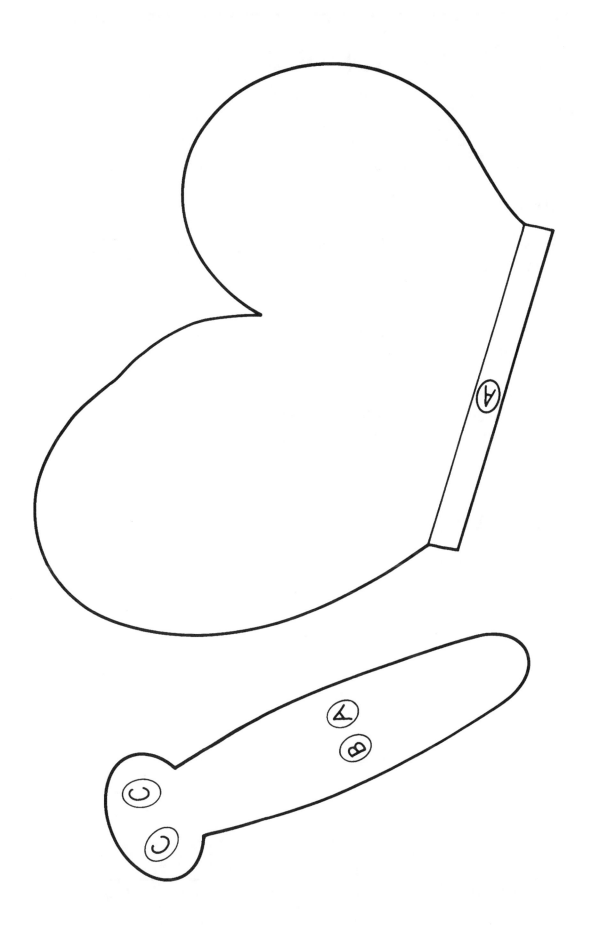

SYMBOL SENSE
Life Roles
"Acceptance of Others"

OBJECTIVES:

1. Students will be able to identify the values of individuals in a group setting.

2. Students will be able to create a symbol that represents positive group interaction.

3. Students will be able to describe how their symbols reflect personal contributions to the group.

SUPPLIES:

Chart paper

PORTFOLIO ENTRY: *Life Roles*, Acceptance of Self and Others, *"Things I've Learned"*

SYMBOL SENSE
Life Roles
"Acceptance of Others"

LESSON	NOTES
1. **Introduction:** Tell students that the lesson will focus on groups and how individuals contribute to group projects.	
2. **Focus:** In large group, ask students to brainstorm qualities that students might bring to a group that is doing a creative project. Suggestions might include: organization, ideas, artistry, sense of color, sense of design, sense of balance. Write their suggestions on chart paper.	
3. **Activity:** Assign small groups. Have students discuss the positive qualities they each bring to the group and then create a visual symbol for their group that represents it. Remind them that they must present the finished product to the class and point out how each member of the group is contained in the symbol. Share the finished product in the large group.	
4. **Closure:** Ask: What did you learn from this lesson? How can this be applied to other situations? Why is it important to value each member of a group?	
5. **Follow-up:** Display the groups' symbols on a bulletin board to show the values of cooperation. Also: Use metaphors and/or similes to describe the cooperative group and other meaningful groups (e.g., family, peer group, extended family, etc.).	

TOUCH AND GO
Life Roles
"Assertiveness Skills"

OBJECTIVES:

1. Students will be able to define appropriate and inappropriate touch.

2. Students will be able to identify examples of appropriate and inappropriate touch.

3. Students will know the proper procedure to follow when dealing with inappropriate touching.

SUPPLIES:

"Three Faces" handouts (provided)

Pictures from a magazine showing people appropriately touching each other

VARIATION:

"Three Faces" handouts without explanations are provided for teachers to use in a group situation where students work co-operatively to provide their own explanations of the three types of touch.

PORTFOLIO ENTRY: *Life Roles,* Competency Skills, *"Interaction with Others"*

TOUCH AND GO
Life Roles
"Assertiveness Skills"

LESSON	NOTES

1. **Introduction:** Show students magazine pictures of people appropriately touching each other (e.g., shaking hands, hugging, patting on the back, etc.). Ask students to guess the probable feelings of the people, based on how they are reacting.

2. **Focus:** Use the handout to show students the "happy" face and explain that this picture is an example of "good" touch. (See explanation of "good touch" on the handout.) Show students the sad face and explain that "bad" touch hurts. Have them give examples. Explain that "confusing" touch is when someone touches them on their bodies in the private places that are covered when wearing a swimming suit.

3. **Activity:** Tell students that when bad touch or confusing touch happens, it is never their fault. If it happens there is a three-step procedure to follow.
   1) Say in a loud, strong voice, "Stop! I don't like that. Don't ever do that again!"
   2) Walk away.
   3) Report it to someone you trust.
   Have students repeat this all together and ask for volunteers to repeat it in pairs and individually.

4. **Closure:** Ask: What did you learn about touching? What do you do when you are touched in a confusing way? Who are your trusted people? Why is it important to report confusing touch?

THREE FACES—TOUCH

GOOD TOUCH is touch that is wanted by both people. It brings out happy feelings, gives information, or is helpful to the person.

BAD TOUCH is touch that one person doesn't want. It hurts, and brings out feelings of hurt or injury.

CONFUSING TOUCH is touch that is done to the private parts of the body, using tricks, threats, or bribes. It may not hurt, but it brings out feelings of confusion, guilt, and embarrassment.

THREE FACES—TOUCH
(without explanations)

GOOD TOUCH

BAD TOUCH

CONFUSING TOUCH

ASSERT YOURSELF
Life Roles
"Assertiveness Skills"

OBJECTIVES:

1. Students will be able to define appropriate and inappropriate conversation.

2. Students will be able to identify examples of appropriate and inappropriate conversation.

3. Students will know the proper procedure to follow when dealing with inappropriate conversation.

SUPPLIES:

"Three Faces—Talk" handouts (provided)

VARIATION:

"Three Faces" handouts without explanations are provided for teachers to use in a group situation where students work co-operatively to provide their own explanations of the three types of assertiveness.

PORTFOLIO ENTRY: *Life Roles,* Competency Skills, *"Interaction with Others"*

ASSERT YOURSELF
Life Roles
"Assertiveness Skills"

LESSON	NOTES

1. **Introduction:** Tell students that the topic of the lesson for the day is appropriate conversation. Recall the lesson on appropriate touching. (See "Touch and Go" Lesson.)

2. **Focus:** Tell students that just as there "good," "bad," and "confusing" touches, likewise, there are "good," "bad," and "confusing" ways to talk. (See handout sheet.) Explain each in sequence. Explain that in order for the topic of conversation to be appropriate, it must pass the 3W test—who, where, what. Give an example of each. The words spoken must suit who the people involved are, where they are talking, and what the consequences might be.

3. **Activity:** When inappropriate talk is heard, it offends people and should not be tolerated. The proper procedure in dealing with it follows:

   1) Ask the person to stop the inappropriate talk because it is offensive or is hurting feelings.

   2) If it doesn't stop, report it to the person in charge (e.g., teacher, bus driver, lunchroom aide).

   3) If the conversation continues, report it to a higher authority (e.g., principal, school counselor, etc.).

   In groups of three, have students make up a skit that shows the proper use of assertiveness skills. Ask for volunteers to perform for the class.

4. **Closure:** Ask: When can you use this assertiveness skill? Why should we use it? What name do we give inappropriate conversation (harassment)? Is reporting incidents being a "snitch"? How can anyone avoid using inappropriate conversation? Why is that important to do?

101

THREE FACES—TALK

GOOD TALK is conversation that is informative, gives directions, is helpful, kind, and positive. It brings feelings of satisfaction, kindness, and warmth.

BAD TALK is conversation that hurts. It degrades, insults, ridicules, lies, or exaggerates.

CONFUSING TALK is conversation that is inappropriate for the people involved, in the places it is done, and for the surrounding audience. It may include talk about body parts or functions. It brings out feelings of embarrassment and guilt.

THREE FACES—TALK
(without explanations)

GOOD TALK

BAD TALK

CONFUSING TALK

VOWEL PLAY
Life Roles
"Assertiveness Skills"

OBJECTIVES:

1. Students will be able to identify reactions and feelings as they respond to conflict.

2. Students will be able to label their reactions and feelings into five categories.

3. Students will be able to identify their most frequent use of each response to conflict.

SUPPLIES:

"Vowel Play" worksheet for each student

PORTFOLIO ENTRY: *Life Roles,* Acceptance of Self and Others, *"Things I've Learned"*

VOWEL PLAY
Life Roles
"Assertiveness Skills"

LESSON	NOTES

1. **Introduction:** Explain that the lesson will focus on conflict, and how students typically respond to it.

2. **Focus:** Pass out the worksheet and ask students to answer the two sections entitled, "WHAT I DO," and "HOW I FEEL." After 10 minutes, have students share their responses in a large group setting.

3. **Activity:** As students share, label each response with one of the following letters based on the content. Tell students to write the letter next to their response. Do not inform the students of the meaning of the letters.

   A—angry and aggressive

   E—evading the conflict, ignoring or walking away

   I—an "I" response (e.g., "I feel")

   O—an opening for the other person, "How do you feel?"

   U—a unifying statement, (e.g., "We can work it out together.")

   Encourage the students to figure out what the letters indicate. Have them count the number of responses for each letter. Inform them of the meaning if they cannot figure it out.

4. **Closure:** Ask: What does this tell you about your responses to conflict situations? Are you satisfied with these responses? Do your responses make the conflict better or worse? What responses might be more effective?

5. **Follow-up:** Ask students to give examples of alternative methods to respond to aggressive conflict situations that might be more effective.

Name _____ **Date** _____

VOWEL PLAY WORKSHEET

CONFLICT SITUATION	WHAT I DO		HOW I FEEL
1. When someone blames me for something I didn't do …			
2. When someone puts me down or makes fun of me …			
3. When someone tells me to do something I don't want to do …			
4. When someone avoids me and appears to be angry or upset with me …			
5. When someone talks behind my back and says things that are lies …			
6. When someone tries to get me involved in a disagreement with others …			
7. When the teacher asks me to do something I know I can't do …			
8. When I am upset with a friend because he/she broke a promise …			
9. When I have a joint project that the other person won't seem to get involved with …			

Name **Leslie**   Date **January 15**

VOWEL PLAY WORKSHEET

CONFLICT SITUATION	WHAT I DO		HOW I FEEL
1. When someone blames me for something I didn't do …	sulk	E	awful
2. When someone puts me down or makes fun of me …	tell them off	A	mad
3. When someone tells me to do something I don't want to do …	ask why	I	confused
4. When someone avoids me and appears to be angry or upset with me…	avoid them	E	upset
5. When someone talks behind my back and says things that are lies …	talk about them	A	mad
6. When someone tries to get me involved in a disagreement with others …	I say no	I/E	in the middle
7. When the teacher asks me to do something I know I can't do …	I ask why	I	dumb
8. When I am upset with a friend because he/she broke a promise …	ask what happened	O	afraid
9. When I have a joint project that the other person won't seem to get	stop working	A	unfair

OBJECTIVES:

1. Students will be able to identify five methods of responding to conflict.

2. Students will be able to distinguish the differing results when using each method.

3. Students will be able to anticipate the possible escalation and de-escalation of conflict when each method is used in response to conflict.

SUPPLIES:

Chart paper

"Vowel Play Skits" handout

VOWEL PLAY CONTINUED
Life Roles
"Assertiveness Skills"

LESSON	NOTES
1. **Introduction:** Tell students that the lesson will review five methods of responding to conflict. (Review the previous "Vowel Play" lesson.)	

2. **Focus:** Ask students to think of conflict situations when they responded using one method and, in hindsight, know that another method would have been more successful.

3. **Activity:** Ask for volunteers to role play the "Vowel Play Skits." (Pass out skits.) After a brief private practice, have students perform them one skit at a time. After each response, have students label each sentence A, E, I, O, or U. Chart each on an escalator to determine whether each sentence escalated or de-escalated the conflict. Use arrows to show the rise or fall of the conflict. Discuss the responses and have students react to each response by the characters.

Example

4. **Closure:** Ask: What did you learn from this lesson? What is the importance of this lesson? Why is it important to use "I", "O," and "U" responses to conflict? Are "A" and "E" responses ever appropriate? Why?

VOWEL PLAY SKITS

Jo and Pat

Jo: Hi, Pat! (friendly slap on the back). How's it going?

Pat: Get your hands off me.

Jo: Well, excuse me for being friendly!

Pat: Shut up, or I'll close that mouth for you!

Casey and Toni

Casey: We're never going to get this project done unless you start doing something on it.

Toni: It's not my fault if the library didn't have the books we needed. What was I supposed to do?

Casey: You're right. I'm just so nervous about this grade.

Toni: We've always done well in the past. Let's ask the teacher for some help.

Lee and Rae

Lee: Don't you know how to ask before you take something?

Rae: You said I could borrow your clothes as long as I return them clean and hung up.

Lee: Well, the deal is off.

Rae: Could you tell me what I've done to upset you?

VOWEL PLAY SKITS (CONTINUED)

Sal and Jodie

Sal: Jodie, you're such a jerk. Kip told me you blabbed about what happened in math class today.

Jodie: I just told the facts.

Sal: Now everybody thinks I'm a loser.

Jodie: Hey, don't take things so seriously.

Penny and Kelly

Penny: It's your turn to do the dishes.

Kelly: Buzz off!

Penny: It's not fair if you don't share some of the responsibility.

Kelly: So, life isn't always fair!

Chris and Jamie

Chris: Jamie, tell Amanda how mean she's acting.

Jamie: I'm not getting involved in your argument.

Chris: But she needs to hear it from somebody else besides me.

Jamie: Maybe if you used kinder words to disagree with her, she'd listen to you.

FUN TIMES
Life Roles
"Use of Leisure Time"

OBJECTIVES:

1. Students will be able to enumerate six activities they enjoy doing in their leisure time.

2. Students will be able to group activities into general categories.

3. Students will be able to visualize which activity is most popular with their peers.

SUPPLIES:

"Fun Times" worksheet

Chart paper

PORTFOLIO ENTRY: *Life Roles,* In My Spare Time, *"What I Prefer"*

FUN TIMES
Life Roles
"Use of Leisure Time"

LESSON	NOTES
1. **Introduction:** Tell students that the lesson will be about activities that they enjoy doing in their spare or leisure time.	
2. **Focus:** Ask students to write the names or draw pictures of their six most favorite leisure-time activities in the boxes on the worksheet. Allow 20 minutes. Cut out each box.	
3. **Activity:** In a large group setting, tell students that leisure-time activities fall into general categories, e.g., sports, arts and crafts, indoor games, entertainment, outside play. (Add others as needed.) Post these categories on large sheets of chart paper. As students share, have them glue their words/pictures under the appropriate category. Make a group decision as to which category is the most popular.	
4. **Closure:** Ask: What did we learn from this activity? Why is it important to talk about leisure time? How were your choices different from your classmates? If an activity does not fit in the "most popular" category, does it make that activity less fun? Do you think your teacher would make the same choices?	
5. **Follow-up:** Suggest that students do the same activity with their parents or siblings. Have them compare the choices with their own. Ask: Why do you think the choices are different?	

FUN TIMES WORKSHEET

Directions: Draw a picture or write about your favorite spare time or leisure activity. Cut the boxes apart when you are finished.

FUN TIMES WORKSHEET

Directions: Draw a picture or write about your favorite spare time or leisure activity. Cut the boxes apart when you are finished.

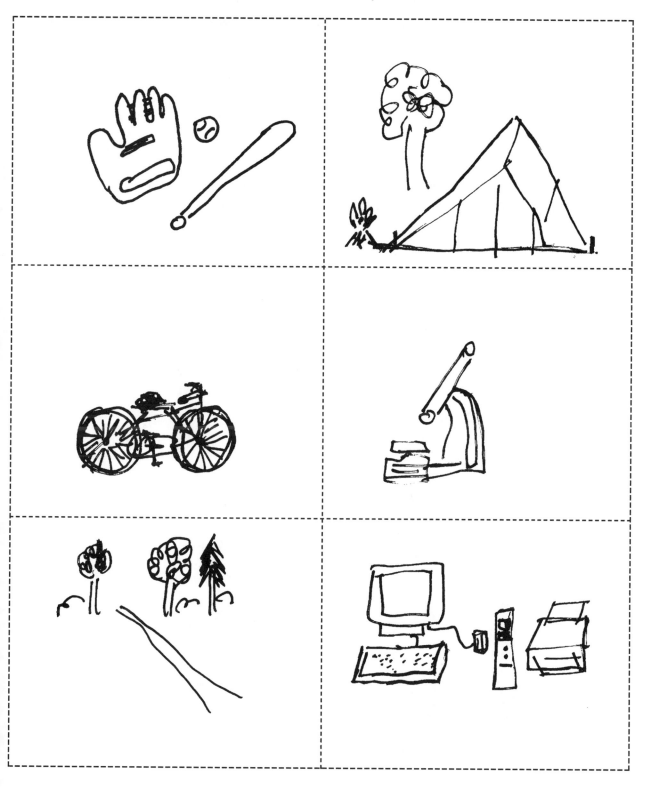

JOB JAR
Life Roles
"Use of Leisure Time"

OBJECTIVES:

1. Students will be able to appreciate the value of using leisure time productively.

2. Students will be able to generate classroom tasks that can be accomplished during earned leisure time.

3. Students will be able to chart their valuable contributions to the class community.

SUPPLIES:

See-through jar or container

Slips of paper

JOB JAR
Life Roles
"Use of Leisure Time"

LESSON	NOTES
1. **Introduction:** Ask students if they have noticed whether all students finish classroom work at the same time. Have students share their feelings about what they do when they wait for others (or have time to spare).	
2. **Focus:** Tell students that this activity will eliminate wasting leisure time.	
3. **Activity:** Ask students to brainstorm, in small groups, quiet and nondisruptive activities that could be done during leisure time while others complete class work. Remind them that all activities must meet with the approval of the teacher in charge of the class. Have them write their suggestions on slips of paper, and after teacher approval, collect them in a clear jar or container. Students will use suggestions from the jar during their spare time for five days and then evaluate how well it's working.	
4. **Closure:** Ask: Why is it important to have a plan for leisure time activities? How does this plan contribute to the class community? Do you think it will work? What problems might the class have with it?	
5. **Follow-up:** Have students evaluate the plan. Add additional suggestions to the jar. Ask students for suggestions to improve the plan. Also: Have students brainstorm activities they could do at home in leisure time.	

TAKE TEN
Life Roles
"Use of Leisure Time"

OBJECTIVES:

1. Students will be able to define leisure time.

2. Students will be able to list leisure-time activities.

3. Students will be able to commit to a daily schedule for involvement in preferred leisure activities.

SUPPLIES:

Dictionary

Sheets of paper

"Take Ten" Goal sheet (one for each student)

PORTFOLIO ENTRY: *Life Roles,* In My Spare Time, *"Extracurricular Activities"*

TAKE TEN

Life Roles

"Use of Leisure Time"

LESSON	NOTES
1. **Introduction:** Tell students that the topic for the lesson is leisure time. Have students define it, using a dictionary if necessary.	
2. **Focus:** Have students list twenty activities they do in their leisure time.	
3. **Activity:** Have students share their lists in small groups and choose three activities that they'd like to spend more time on. Ask students to choose one activity to which they could reasonably commit ten minutes a day. Share the decision in a large group setting and have them make a written commitment to do it. (See "Take Ten" Goal sheet.) Have each student choose a classmate who will act as an "encourager," to help him or her commit to this goal for five days.	
4. **Closure:** Ask: Did you enjoy your commitment? What difficulties did you experience? What did you learn about committing to a leisure-time goal? What effect did your "encourager" have on your success? Do you plan to continue your activity? Would you make such a commitment again?	

"TAKE TEN" GOAL SHEET

I commit to spend 10 minutes a day for five days doing

_____

_____

_____

_____

_____

My encourager will be _____

Name _____ **Date** _____

Sample student goal sheet

"TAKE TEN" GOAL SHEET

I commit to spend 10 minutes a day for five days doing

running or jogging

My encourager will be **Ryan**

Name **Kyle**   Date **May 1, 1996**

> Other typical responses:
> practice baseball
> practice instrument
> learn trick with a yo-yo
> dance
> draw cartoons
> skateboard
> paint
> read
> garden

CHAPTER SIX

Start Your Engines

Lessons to Promote Educational Development

Students can learn that their educational development is like tuning the engine of a car. If great care and attention have been put into both the design and the assembly of that engine, as well as the proper maintenance, then the vehicle should run smoothly. Students are also acutely aware that if they plan to drive a car one day, they need to complete an approved driver education course. Knowing the rules of the road helps one to be a safe driver. It's helpful if we learn some defensive driving skills, too.

A driver education course starts with the basics, and moves to the more advanced skills needed to handle a car responsibly. Even simple tasks like how to turn the key in the ignition, how to put the car in gear, how and when to step on the accelerator, and how to step on the brake are all given attention in the early sessions. Of course, lots of us knew how to do these things before the driver education class, but the course is to make sure everyone knows the basics. Students' educational development is no different. The relevance of one's education needs to be reinforced often, so that students see the relationship of their education to their success in life. The educational basics need to attend to readiness factors (turning the key in the ignition), classifying learning experiences (putting it in gear), finding sources of motivation (stepping on the accelerator), and recognizing limitations and challenges (stepping on the brakes).

Advanced drivers still need to continue learning as they mature. That's why automobile clubs send out magazines with tips for driving in hazardous weather, as well as research reports that enlighten us about safety issues, traffic statistics, and driving preferences. And when it comes to life's journeys, they also let us know about some great vacation opportunities!

Even race car drivers find it necessary to be well educated if they are to be successful. They use a combination of their knowledge and their experience to run a better race. They also learn from their mistakes. Racers and their pit crews always have a checklist of items to verify before a race to make sure every part is in working order. The concept of lifelong learning has many role models and metaphors.

In this chapter, the lessons on educational development are designed to help students appreciate and invest in their educational opportunities as they seek career fulfillment. The five components of Educational Development that are addressed are: Thinking and Learning, Assessment Skills, Work Habits, Social and Economic Foundations, and Academic Planning. Educational development in the career decision-making process is like having smart drivers and cars with well-tuned engines. If everything is in working order, the engine should start the first time and keep running smoothly, with only occasional stops for refueling and minor maintenance.

OBJECTIVES:

1. Students will be able to participate in three activities that are specifically visual, auditory, and kinesthetic.

2. Students will be able to assess their most comfortable style of learning.

3. Students will be able to identify how they can apply visual, auditory, and kinesthetic skills to academic situations.

SUPPLIES:

10 small items

Tray

Paper

Pencils

"Learning Sense" Activities sheet

LEARNING SENSE
Educational Development
"Thinking and Learning"

LESSON	NOTES
1. **Introduction:** Tell students that in the next four lessons, they will participate in activities that use specific senses to learn.	
2. **Focus:** Tell students that each activity focuses on one of the following senses: seeing, hearing, or touching.	
3. **Activities:** (See following pages.) Lesson 1—Concentration Lesson 2—Let's Go Shopping Lesson 3—Back Scratch Lesson 4—Follow-up	
4. **Closure:** After each lesson, ask: What thinking or learning skill was most important for you to be successful at this lesson? How do you use this skill when you learn in school?	
5. **Follow-up:** Ask: Which lesson did you enjoy the most? Why? Which one was the hardest? Why? What school subjects use these skills? How can these activities give you hints about learning better? List subjects that use one sense more than the others. How well do you do?	

LEARNING SENSE ACTIVITIES

VISUAL

Teacher Preparation:

Concentration

Select 10 or more small objects (e.g., a marble, button, crayon, lock, etc.) and place them on a tray. Have students study the objects and try to remember them. Ask students to close their eyes, then remove one or more objects from the tray. When presented with the tray, ask students to identify the missing object(s). Continue several times and increase difficulty.

AUDITORY

Let's Go Shopping

Ask students to listen carefully while you read a shopping list. Ask for volunteers to repeat the list. Increase the size of the list, or ask for the list to be repeated in reverse order for added difficulty.

List 1	*List 2*	*List 3*
bread	bologna	catsup
milk	lettuce	vinegar
pickles	motor oil	candy
rice	cat food	toothbrush
	raisins	yogurt
	film	walnuts
		meat
		postcard
		ice cream

Let's try one more time with some other shopping lists to remember. See if you can do better than last time.

List 1	*List 2*	*List 3*
soap	sliced ham	oranges
chocolate milk	juice	shampoo
spaghetti	crackers	newspaper
apples	peanut butter	toothpaste
	rice	applesauce
	green beans	cheese
		muffins
		popcorn

LEARNING SENSE ACTIVITIES (CONTINUED)

Back Scratch

Pair students (A and B). Have B sit behind A. Pass a design (below) to B. Have B draw the design with a finger on A's back. A, in turn, will draw what he or she feels on paper. Compare the results. Switch roles.

PERFECT DAY
Educational Development
"Thinking and Learning"

OBJECTIVES:

1. Students will be able to list activities that would make a perfect day.

2. Students will be able to categorize each activity as visual, auditory, or kinesthetic.

3. Students will be able to enumerate thinking and learning skills needed to complete the activity and identify personal preferences.

SUPPLIES:

"Perfect Day" worksheet

PORTFOLIO ENTRY: *Educational Development*, Learning Assets, *"Things I've Learned"*

PERFECT DAY
Educational Development
"Thinking and Learning"

LESSON	NOTES
1. **Introduction:** Tell students that thinking and learning are very personal and individual.	
2. **Focus:** Tell students that they will have the opportunity to think, and plan a perfect day.	
3. **Activity:** In a large group, brainstorm a few possible activities that might take place on a perfect day. Then ask students to individually plan out their specific choices in one-hour blocks. Students may work in pairs to stimulate creativity. In the large group, have students share their choices. When that is completed, have them review their lists and label each activity according to whether they use their eyes, ears, or body to do the activity. Some may be labeled with more than one. Give examples for clarification. Total each category at the bottom of the worksheet.	
4. **Closure:** Ask: What was the easiest part of planning the day? What was the most difficult part? What did you learn by labeling the choices? Is this a true indication of who you are?	
5. **Follow-up:** Ask students to have their parents plan a perfect day for them. Compare the list and ask: How are the perfect days different? Why? What did you learn about your parents?	

_____'S PERFECT DAY WORKSHEET
(student name)

TIME	ACTIVITY	CATEGORY
	Get up	
	Go to bed	

CATEGORY TALLY

Eyes ____   Ears ____   Body ____

_____'S PERFECT DAY WORKSHEET

TIME	ACTIVITY	CATEGORY
7:00	Get up — omelet for breakfast	Body
8:00	Call friends — plan day	Ears
9:00	Go buy new computer with tons of cool software	Eyes, body
10:00	Play games on computer	Eyes
11:00	Get ready to go to lunch (travel)	Body
12:00	Meet Michael Jordan for lunch	Body, eyes, ears
1:00	Play some hoops with Michael, get his autograph	Body
2:00	Meet some friends at the pool	Body
3:00	Go buy some new CDs	Ears, eyes
4:00	Come home — learn that I got all As on my report card!	Eyes
5:00	Go out to eat at my favorite restaurant	Body
6:00	Still at restaurant eating dessert	Body
7:00	See an awesome movie	Eyes
	↓	
9:00	Go home	Body
9:30	Go to bed	Body

CATEGORY TALLY

Eyes __6__   Ears __3__   Body ____

OBJECTIVES:

1. Students will be able to list daily school activities and rate their enjoyment of each.

2. Students will be able to categorize each activity as auditory, visual, or kinesthetic.

3. Students will be able to compare their enjoyment scale with their learning style preference.

SUPPLIES:

"All in a Day's Work" worksheet

ALL IN A DAY'S WORK
Educational Development
"Thinking and Learning"

LESSON	NOTES
1. **Introduction:** Tell students that this activity will be very individual and personal.	
2. **Focus:** Tell students that the activity focuses on how students learn best in a school setting.	
3. **Activity:** Pass out worksheet, and ask students to list twenty activities they do at school on a regular basis. Then, have them rate each activity as Awesome—4, Enjoy—3, Rather Not—2, or Bummer—1. When that is completed, define and discuss activities that are visual, auditory, and kinesthetic. Now ask them to go back and categorize each activity as visual, auditory, or kinesthetic. (Some activities may fall into two categories.) Tally each learning style by adding the enjoyment score numbers and placing the total at the bottom of the sheet.	
4. **Closure:** Ask: What did you learn about learning and enjoyment of school activities? How can you use this knowledge to become a better learner? How did this lesson challenge your thinking skills?	

ALL IN A DAY'S WORK
WORKSHEET

Directions: List 20 activities you do at school

	SCORE	CATEGORY
1.		
2.		
3.		
4.		
5.		
6.		
7.		
8.		
9.		
10.		
11.		
12.		
13.		
14.		
15.		
16.		
17.		
18.		
19.		
20.		

SCORING	CATEGORY	TOTALS
4 - Awesome	A Auditory	Auditory _____
3 - Enjoy	V Visual	Visual _____
2 - Rather Not	K Kinesthetic	Kinesthetic _____
1 - Bummer		

Name _____ **T.J.** _____

ALL IN A DAY'S WORK WORKSHEET

Directions: List 20 activities you do at school

		SCORE	CATEGORY
1.	Play tag	4	K
2.	Line up	1	K
3.	Do penmanship	2	K/V
4.	Correct spelling	2	A
5.	Eat snack	4	K
6.	Do math	4	K
7.	Make lunch list	4	V/K
8.	Silent read	3	V
9.	Do science experiment	4	V/K
10.	Recess	4	K
11.	Play Uno	3	V/K
12.	Help in Kitchen	4	K
13.	Writing workshop	2	K/V
14.	Run errands	4	K
15.	Collect garbage	4	K
16.	Show and tell	3	V/K
17.			
18.			
19.			
20.			

SCORING	CATEGORY	TOTALS	
4 - Awesome	A Auditory	Auditory	**2**
3 - Enjoy	V Visual	Visual	**21**
2 - Rather Not	K Kinesthetic	Kinesthetic	**47**
1 - Bummer			

OBJECTIVES:

1. Students will be able to identify criteria for quality work relative to an art project.

2. Students will be able to apply these criteria to a self-portrait.

3. Students will be able to apply the concept of personal growth and assessment to academic areas.

SUPPLIES:

Drawing paper

Crayons

Pencils

PICTURE PERFECT
Educational Development
"Assessment Skills"

LESSON	NOTES
1. **Introduction:** Ask students to think about (or show them an example of) a portrait that is of good quality.	
2. **Focus:** Ask them to brainstorm "criteria" or standards necessary for the work to have in order to be considered "good." Chart their suggestions. Examples may include: clarity, color, form, identifiable characteristics, etc. Write the examples on chart paper and judge the work as follows: 4 perfect 3 good 2 fair 1 poor	
3. **Activity:** Ask students to keep these criteria in mind as they draw a self-portrait. Adequate time should be allowed for students to complete their work. Then ask them to critique their own portraits by rating them based on the criteria given earlier. Discuss the value of self-assessment.	
4. **Closure:** Ask: Was it difficult to critique your own work? Why? What was the purpose of this lesson? In what other ways do we make self-assessments? What criteria do we use in making these other self-assessments? How will this experience be useful to you in the future?	
5. **Follow-up:** Save the original portraits and have students draw another later on in the school year. Apply the same criteria to the latter picture.	

Educational Development

"Assessment Skills"

OBJECTIVES:

1. Students will be able to specify subjects that are difficult and easy for them to learn.

2. Students will be able to enumerate the reasons why they find subjects difficult and easy.

3. Students will be able to brainstorm strategies to help make the difficult subject matter easier to learn.

SUPPLIES:

"Tough Going" worksheet

"Easy Going" worksheet (duplicate on contrasting colored paper)

Chart paper

Markers

PORTFOLIO ENTRY: *Educational Development,* Assessment Skills, *Achievement*

TOUGH GOING/EASY GOING
Educational Development
"Assessment Skills"

LESSON	NOTES

1. **Introduction:** Tell students that they will have the opportunity to assess their academic strengths and challenges.

2. **Focus:** Let students know that because they are unique individuals, they may find certain subject matters more difficult than others to learn. Today's lesson will concentrate on ways to improve the difficult ones. List four or five major subject areas of the grade level.

3. **Activity:** Give each student both worksheets. At the top of the Tough Going worksheet, have them write the name of the subject they find most difficult, and suggest at least three reasons why it is difficult. On the Easy Going worksheet, have them name the subject they find the easiest, and suggest at least three reasons why. When that is complete, survey the class subjects. Group students by threes or fours according to the subject they find most difficult. Have each group brainstorm five methods for improvement. (Examples may include: getting help from a friend or parent, asking more questions in class, doing extra examples, re-reading assignments, having an adult check homework, exercising more care in doing the work.) Have each small group report and display a list of their suggestions.

4. **Closure:** Ask: What was the purpose of this lesson? When will it be useful to you? How can you improve in your most difficult subject? Which suggestions would be helpful to you? Is it important to set a goal for your difficult subjects? Who would you share your goal with? How could you evaluate your improvement?

TOUGH GOING WORKSHEET

The subject I find the hardest in school is _____

because:

1. _____
   _____
   _____

2. _____
   _____
   _____

3. _____
   _____
   _____

Name _____ **Date** _____

EASY GOING WORKSHEET

The subject I find easiest in school is _____

because:

1. _____
   _____
   _____

2. _____
   _____
   _____

3. _____
   _____
   _____

BEST TESTERS
Educational Development
"Assessment Skills"

OBJECTIVES:

1. Students will be able to reduce test anxiety by pre-test exploration and exercises.

2. Students will be able to view testing situations in a positive, controlled manner.

3. Students will be able to apply test-taking strategies to other stressful situations.

SUPPLIES:

"Best Tester" Cheer sheets (provided)

Chart paper

BEST TESTERS
Educational Development
"Assessment Skills"

LESSON	NOTES
1. **Introduction:** Tell students that this lesson and the following lesson will be about tests and test taking.	
2. **Focus:** Ask how many students plan to drive a car, pilot a plane, become an electrician, teach young children, etc. (or any other profession that requires a test to determine competence). Tell them that all require tests. How do you feel before, during, and after tests?	
3. **Activity:** Tell students that you are going to discuss two different ways to prepare for tests. One way is to review the information that will be covered on the test; the other is to prepare your attitude. When you do both, you become a "Best Tester." The first two rules of becoming a "Best Tester" are: 1. Get rest the night before the test and eat a good breakfast in the morning. (Discuss the value of each. Write the rule on chart paper). 2. Arrest the stress. (Discuss how stress can affect the thinking and achieving process.) To relieve this stress, breathe deeply, think briefly of a pleasant thought, and get back to the test. (Write the rule on chart paper. After each discussion introduce a cheer. See following pages.)	
4. **Closure:** Ask: What did you learn about test taking? Why is it important? When and how could you apply these rules to other situations?	
5. **Follow-up:** Continue with "Best Testers—Continued" lesson.	

BEST TESTER CHEER 1

We're BEST TESTERS; we're strong. (clap, clap)

We're BEST TESTERS; we rate. (clap, clap)

We eat our breakfasts, get our rest.

We're BEST TESTERS; we're great! (clap, clap)

BEST TESTER CHEER 2

We're going to get our rest. (clap, clap)

We're going to beat the stress. (clap, clap)

We're going to bust the _____. (name the test)

We're BEST TESTERS; we're best. (clap, clap)

BEST TESTERS CONTINUED
Educational Development
"Assessment Skills"

OBJECTIVES:

1. Students will be able to reduce test anxiety by pre-test exploration and exercises.

2. Students will be able to view testing situations in a positive, controlled manner.

3. Students will be able to apply test-taking strategies to other stressful situations.

SUPPLIES:

"Best Tester" Cheers sheet (provided)

Chart paper

Best Tester Badges (provided)

PORTFOLIO ENTRY: *Educational Development,* Work Habits

BEST TESTERS CONTINUED
Educational Development
"Assessment Skills"

LESSON	NOTES

1. **Introduction:** Ask students to recall the previous lesson. Review the first two rules and the cheers. Tell them that there are two more rules to learn before becoming an official "Best Tester."

2. **Focus:** Ask students if they have ever watched a quiz show on television or played one in school. Do the contestants always answer correctly? How do you think they feel when they don't know the answer or answer it incorrectly? Might they get discouraged?

3. **Activity:** Tell students that the third rule to become a "Best Tester" is to keep working—don't get discouraged—because you could find that you know the next answer. Write the rule on chart paper. (Introduce cheer and repeat several times.)

   The last rule of becoming a "Best Tester" is to go at a medium speed and pick out the best answer. You have to take enough time to read the test, but not spend too much time on just a few questions. If the question is very difficult, the strategy to use is to still pick the answer, because some tests have items on them that you haven't been taught yet. The test wants to discover if you have learned the information somewhere else or can figure out the right answer. Write the rule on chart paper. (Introduce another cheer and repeat several times.)

4. **Closure:** Review all the rules and the cheers. Ask students if they can recite the rules from memory. As students show their knowledge of the rules, award them with "Best Tester" badges. Allow them to award each other the badges. Eventually, the entire class will be wearing badges. Ask: Do you think that becoming "Best Testers" is important? How will it help you during the test? How will it help you in the future?

5. **Follow-up:** Check with students during and after the test and ask if they used "Best Tester" strategies. Were they helpful?

BEST TESTER CHEER 3

The_____ (name test)'s a pest, (clap, clap)

But I must do my best. (clap, clap)

I just won't let it get me down

'cause I can beat this test. (clap, clap)

BEST TESTER CHEER 4

There might be stuff that's new, (clap, clap)

Or items hard for you. (clap, clap)

Just work along and do your best

So we can beat this test. (clap, clap)

Don't go too fast or slow. (clap, clap)

Do everything you know. (clap, clap)

Pick up the answer that's the best

So we can beat this test. (clap, clap)

"Best Tester" Badges

OBJECTIVES:

1. Students will be able to participate in a class meeting.

2. Students will be able to identify the skills necessary to complete a task successfully.

3. Students will be able to role play the task and apply it to school situations.

SUPPLIES:

Chart paper

Markers

PORTFOLIO ENTRY: *Educational Development,* Work Habits, *Competency Skills, "Work Relates to Needs"*

LET'S HAVE A MEETING
Educational Development
"Work Habits"

LESSON	NOTES
1. **Introduction:** Tell students that they will be participating in a class meeting.	

1. **Introduction:** Tell students that they will be participating in a class meeting.

2. **Focus:** Tell students that in a class meeting, students will be asked to share their personal ideas on a particular topic. Suggest that many jobs have meetings so that work can be accomplished efficiently and productively.

3. **Activity:** Tell students that a class meeting has three rules:

   1. Raise hands.
   2. Listen to others.
   3. Share ideas only on the topic.

   When students have agreed to follow these rules, announce the topic of the lesson. Topics may include, but not be limited to, student study skills (e.g., completing assignments, listening to directions, working quietly, reading silently, following directions, asking questions, neatness, cooperating in a group, etc.). Place the topic title on chart paper, and write all the brainstormed ideas that students suggest to be successful at the skill. Skills may be expanded to activities outside the classroom (e.g., following directions in the gym, at lunch, in the hall). Ask for volunteers to role play the skill, using the suggestions that have been brainstormed.

4. **Closure:** Ask: What are the rules for a class meeting? Why are the rules important? What was the topic of today's class meeting? What was important about the topic? How will this skill make you a better student? How will this skill make you a better worker in a job?

5. **Follow-up:** Review, practice, and reinforce.

HABIT FORMING
Educational Development
"Work Habits"

OBJECTIVES:

1. Students will be able to identify specific ways to implement a new work habit.

2. Students will be able to commit to using the new work habit in a school setting.

3. Students will be able to identify specific reasonable rewards to reinforce the habit.

SUPPLIES:

Work Habit Contract (provided)

HABIT FORMING
Educational Development
"Work Habits"

LESSON	NOTES
1. **Introduction:** Tell students that good work habits are necessary throughout life.	
2. **Focus:** Brainstorm five or six specific work habits necessary to be a successful student (e.g., neatness, complete answers, organization, doing homework, passing in work on time). Have individual students select one work habit to which they will commit.	
3. **Activity:** Group students by their choices. Have them discuss specific strategies for developing the work habit, and rewards that will reinforce it. Pass out work habit contracts and have students fill them in.	
4. **Closure:** Ask: What is a good work habit? Why are they important to develop? Why is it important to reward your accomplishments? What have you learned from this activity?	

WORK HABITS CONTRACT

_____ will develop this work habit:

_____ .

To do this, I will:

1. _____

2. _____

3. _____

4. _____

My reward: _____

Signed _____

Date _____

Sample Student Contract

WORK HABITS CONTRACT

Cole will develop this work habit: **Improve**
spelling test grade .

To do this, I will:

1. **write words 5 times**

2. **write sentences for each**

3. **get help from parents**

4. **study before the test**

My reward: **fishing with P.J.**

Signed _Cole_

Date _____

Educational Development

"Work Habits"

OBJECTIVES:

1. Students will be able to brainstorm a list of learning and study skills that are necessary to be a successful student.

2. Students will be able to verbalize the problems that they have with each skill.

3. Students will be able to decide whether improvement in the skills can be accomplished by personal effort or with the help of the teacher.

SUPPLIES:

Chart paper

Four different color markers

"No Lobsters" worksheet (provided)

NO LOBSTERS
Educational Development
"Work Habits"

LESSON	NOTES
1. **Introduction:** Tell students that this lesson will investigate some learning skills that they may have already developed to some degree, and could possibly improve.	
2. **Focus:** Show students a chart that has each letter of the words NO LOBSTERS written vertically. Each letter stands for a learning skill that is necessary to develop to become a successful student. As students guess correctly, fill in the answer next to the letter (Note taking, Organization, Listening, Observation, Behavior, Studying, Time management, Exam taking, Reference skills, Style of learning). Discuss each.	
3. **Activity:** Form three evenly-spaced vertical columns after the list of skills. Label each in different colors—PROBLEMS, STUDENT SOLUTIONS, TEACHER SOLUTIONS. (See following page.) Have students identify and chart in small or large groups the problems they have applying each skill, what action students could take to improve the skill, and what a teacher could do to increase the success of each skill.	
4. **Closure:** Ask: What did you learn from this lesson? How could these suggestions improve your study habits?	
5. **Follow-up:** Ask students to prepare for the next lesson by sharing the three skills they find most difficult to master and one goal they could create to improve the skill. Continue with the next lesson, "NO LOBSTERS—Continued."	

Name _____ **Date** _____

NO LOBSTERS

		PROBLEMS	STUDENT SOLUTIONS	TEACHER SOLUTIONS
N	Note Taking			
O	Organization			
L	Listening			
O	Observation			
B	Behavior			
S	Studying			
T	Time Management			
E	Exam Taking			
R	Reference Skills			
S	Style of Learning			

Name *Morgan*

NO LOBSTERS

		PROBLEMS	STUDENT SOLUTIONS	TEACHER SOLUTIONS
N	Note Taking	*can't see too sloppy*	*move ask teacher*	*write neater*
O	Organization			
L	Listening	*too much talking*	*stop it*	*give warnings*
O	Observation	*too loud to concentrate*		
B	Behavior			
S	Studying	*don't have a good place to study*	*find one*	
T	Time Management	*too much homework*	*do a little each night*	*check with other teachers*
E	Exam Taking			
R	Reference Skills			
S	Style of Learning			

NO LOBSTERS CONTINUED
Educational Development
"Work Habits"

OBJECTIVES:

1. Students will become familiar with basic learning skills, problems in developing them, and possible solutions.

2. Students will be able to set at least three goals to improve their learning skills.

3. Students will be able to evaluate which skills would apply to the world of work.

SUPPLIES:

"NO LOBSTERS" chart from previous lesson

Markers

PORTFOLIO ENTRY: *Educational Development,* Work Habits, *Special Needs*

NO LOBSTERS CONTINUED
Educational Development
"Work Habits"

LESSON	NOTES
1. **Introduction:** Ask students to recall the NO LOBSTERS lesson. See if students can list the skills without looking at the chart.	
2. **Focus:** Ask students to individually identify the skill they find to be the most difficult to develop. Group students according to their selection (e. g., all students whose first choice is time management would be in the same group).	
3. **Activity:** Tell groups they have ten minutes to examine why the skill is so difficult for them and to set at least three goals that group members could attempt to improve it. Have each group select a person to report to the large group. Share the in-depth problems and goals. Ask each student in the class to make a written commitment to no more than three goals suggested by the class. Ask for a report of students' progress in a week.	
4. **Closure:** Ask: What was the purpose of this lesson? When have learning skills been discussed before? Who should be responsible to teach students learning skills? Can you remember when you learned any of them? Which skills would be important to have in a job? Are some skills more necessary in certain jobs? Give examples.	
5. **Follow-up:** This lesson can be reviewed periodically throughout the school year. Charts can be devised to show the progress students are making by improved grades or teacher commendations.	

OBJECTIVES:

1. Students will be able to view their city or town as an independent community.

2. Students will be able to investigate the number of services available in their community.

3. Students will be able to recommend services that are needed in the community.

SUPPLIES:

Town reports

Phone numbers of local officials

Chart paper

Markers

PORTFOLIO ENTRY: *Educational Development,* Competency Skills, *"Functions of Society"*

OUR TOWN
Educational Development
"Social and Economic Foundations"

LESSON	NOTES
1. **Introduction:** Tell students that they will be investigating their own community.	
2. **Focus:** Ask students to brainstorm the services and agencies that are needed in a community. Chart their responses and save for reference. Answers may include: banks, stores, schools, industries, leisure-time areas and services (e.g., food stores, gas stations, doctors, counseling services, and welfare agencies). Discuss where they might find this information quickly.	

Part I

3. **Activity:** Assign groups of students the task of counting the number of services available within the confines of the community, or have a knowledgeable community official come to the class as a guest speaker to discuss community services.

Part II

Activity: Have students report on the services available in their community, and chart the results. Compare the results to the original brainstormed list. Have students make recommendations as to the new services needed to make the community self-sufficient.

4. **Closure:** Ask: Why is it important to know your community? What recommendations would you make to your community officials to improve your community and how would you do it? What do you think they will say about your recommendations? How does your education prepare you for contributing to your community?

5. **Follow-up:** Write the class' recommendations in letter form and send the letter to your town officials. Mention the fact that this was a class project and a response would be appreciated.

OUR TOWN CONTINUED
Educational Development
"Social and Economic Foundations"

OBJECTIVES:

1. Students will be able to enumerate the services necessary for a successful community.

2. Students will be able to work cooperatively to plan a model of the town.

3. Students will be able to create a visual representation of the model town.

SUPPLIES:

Milk cartons of varying sizes

Small boxes

Cardboard

Markers

Large sheet of paper

Glue

Scissors

Tape

PORTFOLIO ENTRY: *Educational Development,* Competency Skills, *"Functions of Society"*

OUR TOWN CONTINUED
Educational Development
"Social and Economic Foundations"

LESSON	NOTES

1. **Introduction:** Tell students that they will be creating their own community in a cooperative classroom effort.

2. **Focus:** Ask students to recall the brainstormed list of services and agencies that are needed in a community from the "Our Town" lesson. Refer to their list of recommendations to improve the community.

3. **Activity:** Tell students that they will be creating a milk-carton community based on their recommendations. Divide the students into five or six small groups and assign each a service to plan: industrial, residential, leisure-time areas, business (e.g., shopping centers, banks, offices); services (e.g., markets, social service agencies, churches); transportation and roads. Ask them to elect one representative to serve on a committee to plan the finished community. (Teacher should predetermine the finished size of the milk-carton town, and the amount of time for completion.)

4. **Closure:** Ask: What did you learn from this lesson? What were the easy parts? What were the hard parts? How could we make this lesson better? Would you ever pursue the occupation of a community planner? What interests you about it? What skills learned in school will make you a better community member?

5. **Follow-up:** Invite a community planner to speak to the class. Have students share their experiences. Invite other classes to view the completed model community.

OBJECTIVES:

1. Students will be able to investigate the workings of a fast-food producer.

2. Students will be able to brainstorm the employment skills and training needed to perform specific jobs.

3. Students will be able to compare the methods of production and training to the school setting.

SUPPLIES:

Community resources

Class trip

Research material

Guest speaker or field trip

Chart paper

PORTFOLIO ENTRY: *Educational Development*, Competency Skills, *"Relationship between Work and Learning"*

LIFE IN THE FAST LANE
Educational Development
"Social and Economic Foundations"

LESSON	NOTES
1. **Introduction:** Tell students that in order for fast-food producers to be successful, they must have a system in place that can be duplicated, so that products and services are consistent and efficient, and of the highest quality.	
2. **Focus:** Tell students that they will be investigating the behind-the-scenes workings of a fast-food producer.	
3. **Activity:** Ask students to research a nationally known fast-food producer. Locally-based establishments may be able to provide reference material. A guest speaker or field trip may be arranged. Ask students to compile a list of all the jobs that are necessary to produce the finished product. Examples may include: training, ordering, purchasing, shipping, cooking, serving, cleaning, and cashiering. Ask students to brainstorm the skills needed to complete each task. Chart their responses. Discuss the methods and the amount of time used to train new employees.	
4. **Closure:** Ask: What did you learn from this lesson? Can any methods used in the fast-food industry be applied to education? What are they? Would they be as efficient in a school setting?	
5. **Follow-up:** Research another fast-food chain and compare its procedures and its success with your first researched chain.	

GOAL—DIG IN!
Educational Development
"Academic Planning"

OBJECTIVES:

1. Students will be able to set a class academic goal.

2. Students will be able to enumerate the steps necessary to accomplish the goal.

3. Students will be able to periodically evaluate their progress.

SUPPLIES:

"Footprints" patterns (provided)

Chart paper

Markers

PORTFOLIO ENTRY: *Educational Development,* Competency Skills, *"Relationship between Work and Learning"*

GOAL—DIG IN!
Educational Development
"Academic Planning"

LESSON	NOTES
1. **Introduction:** Tell students that they will be doing a cooperative activity that requires everybody to do their parts in order to accomplish it.	
2. **Focus:** Give students a few examples of an academic class goal, e.g., learning the alphabet, times tables, and state capitols, publishing a summer activity book, creating an information bulletin board, etc.	
3. **Activity:** Once the goal is chosen, brainstorm and chart the steps necessary to complete the task. Prioritize the order. Write each step in a footprint and display in order around the classroom. (Leave space between footprints for unanticipated additions.) As the class "digs in" to the goal, color the toes and put a large check in the foot.	
4. **Closure:** At the completion of the project, ask students to recall the process. Ask: What steps did we forget? Which ones were the hardest to dig in to? Which were easy? Did we build in any rewards along the way? How do you feel about your contribution to the goal? How could this goal be accomplished faster?	
5. **Follow-up:** Suggest students do the same with personal academic goals. Present "Goal—Dig In!—Continued"	

Footprint pattern

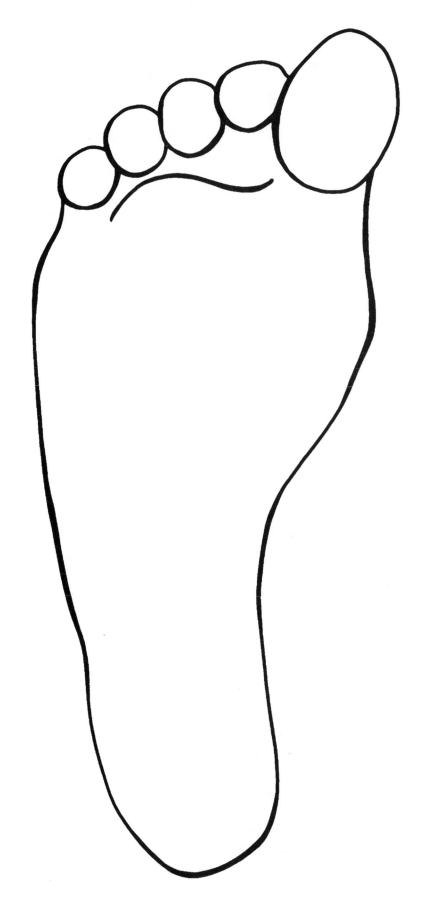

Footprint pattern

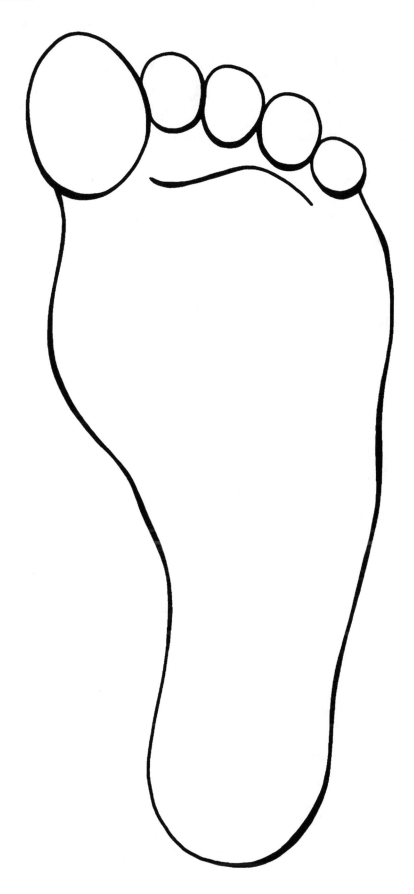

GOAL—DIG IN! CONTINUED
Educational Development
"Academic Planning"

OBJECTIVES:

1. Students will be able to set individual short-term goals that are academic.

2. Students will be able to enumerate the steps necessary to accomplish the goals.

3. Students will be able to periodically evaluate their progress.

SUPPLIES:

"Personal Goal" worksheet

PORTFOLIO ENTRY: *Educational Development,* Work Habits, *Attitudes toward Learning*

GOAL—DIG IN! CONTINUED
Educational Development
"Academic Planning"

LESSON	NOTES

1. **Introduction:** Review the previous lesson, "Goal—Dig In!" and discuss the process of setting a group goal.

2. **Focus:** Tell students that they will each be setting a short-term academic goal.

3. **Activity:** Discuss the difference between setting a group and a personal goal (e.g., total responsibility, lack of group help and encouragement, difficulty level, cooperative effort, and fun). Then, ask students to share academic goal ideas that students at their grade level might attempt. Examples may include: a perfect spelling score, increased journal entry, increased participation in discussions, etc. Have students choose a goal and discuss in pairs. Students may even want to discuss goals with their parents before "digging in." After the selection of the goal is made, group students according to similar goals and have them brainstorm the steps they need to take to accomplish them. Have them number the steps in priority order, and write them on individual footprints on the personal goal worksheets. As steps are accomplished, have students color them. When goals are completed, display the worksheets on a bulletin board.

4. **Closure:** After a reasonable period of time, ask students: What steps did you forget? Which were easy? Which were hard? What would have made your goal easier? How did you feel when you accomplished your goal? Can you set a new goal using similar steps? How can you accomplish an incomplete goal?

173

PERSONAL GOAL WORKSHEET

My goal is _____

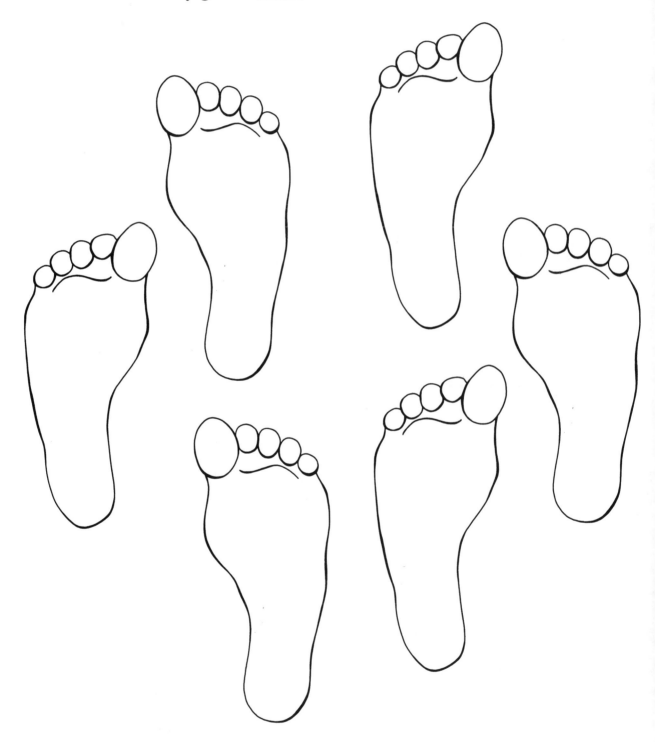

Name   *Marty* _____   Date _____

PERSONAL GOAL WORKSHEET

My goal is   *Read 2 books this month.* _____

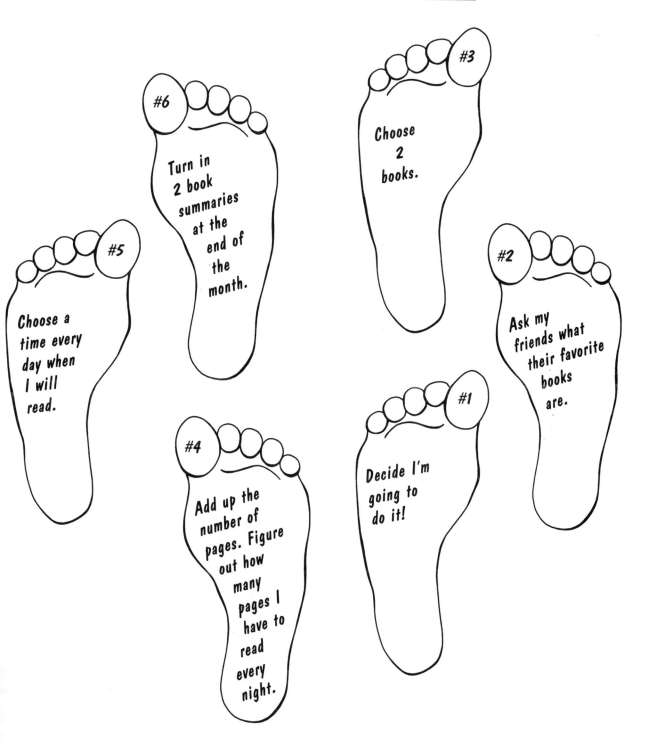

#6 Turn in 2 book summaries at the end of the month.

#3 Choose 2 books.

#5 Choose a time every day when I will read.

#2 Ask my friends what their favorite books are.

#4 Add up the number of pages. Figure out how many pages I have to read every night.

#1 Decide I'm going to do it!

GET A JOB?
Educational Development
"Academic Planning"

OBJECTIVES:

1. Students will be able to choose a career interest area.

2. Students will be able to investigate educational training requirements for one specific career choice.

3. Students will be able to determine academic courses necessary to meet a basic entry-level position.

SUPPLIES:

Career resources from the library, such as:
- *Dictionary of Occupational Titles*
- Vocational computer software
- Occupational encyclopedia

"Get a Job" worksheet

Chart paper

Markers

Guest speaker

PORTFOLIO ENTRY: *Educational Development,* Competency Skills, *"Educational Programs"*

GET A JOB?
Educational Development
"Academic Planning"

LESSON	NOTES
1. **Introduction:** Tell students that career choices fall into clusters due to a particular occupation's primary focus on certain kinds of work.	

2. **Focus:** These clusters are: Business and Office; Marketing and Distribution; Communication and Media; Construction; Manufacturing; Fine Arts and Humanities; Health; Recreation and Hospitality; Personal/Public Service; Transportation; Agricultural Business and Natural Resources; Marine Science and Environment; and Consumer and Homemaking Services. Ask students to brainstorm particular professions that might be included in each cluster. Categorize on chart paper.

3. **Activity:** Ask students to choose one cluster and investigate one occupation in that cluster of particular interest to them. Ask them to focus on the entry-level requirements for the position. Pass out and explain the worksheet. Give students an ample amount of time to do the research. Encourage the use of computer software and library resources, if available.

4. **Closure:** Ask: What did you learn from this investigation? What resources did you use? Were they readily available to you? Did your interest in your occupational choice increase or decrease? Why? How does this lesson affect your future educational choices?

5. **Follow-up:** Invite guest speakers who hold various positions to discuss their job's entry-level requirements and whether there are circumstances under which those requirements are altered.

GET A JOB WORKSHEET

NAME: _____

OCCUPATIONAL CLUSTER: _____

OCCUPATIONAL CHOICE: _____

ENTRY-LEVEL REQUIREMENTS:

1. _____

2. _____

3. _____

4. _____

5. _____

_____

_____

_____

REVIEW EACH REQUIREMENT AND DO THE FOLLOWING:

—Put a slash (/) through the number of any requirement already completed.

—Put a circle (O) around any number that can be completed with further education or training.

—Put a question mark (?) next to any number that you cannot respond to.

—Blacken any number (•) for which you will be unable to meet entry-level requirements.

GET A JOB WORKSHEET

NAME: _____

OCCUPATIONAL CLUSTER: _____

OCCUPATIONAL CHOICE: _____

ENTRY-LEVEL REQUIREMENTS:

① _____

② _____

③ _____

4̸. _____

⑤ **coursework in computer science, geography, foreign language**
and history preferred

_____

_____

REVIEW EACH REQUIREMENT AND DO THE FOLLOWING:

—Put a slash (/) through the number of any requirement already completed.

—Put a circle (O) around any number that can be completed with further education or training.

—Put a question mark (?) next to any number that you cannot respond to.

—Blacken any number (•) for which you will be unable to meet entry-level requirements.

CHAPTER SEVEN

The Roadmap

Lessons to Foster Career Exploration and Planning

If you know where you're starting and you know your destination, then the roadmap targets all the trails that need to be taken to get you where you want to go. One's career requires a road atlas. The traveler needs to have a global view of what's ahead, but also needs to know how many separate but interconnecting trips might be required to really "see the world" in perspective and make it a truly rewarding journey.

Career decisions are not little day trips, although some day trips (like job shadowing) can provide major insights about what to avoid in the future and what you want to be sure to include in future trips. There are no simple roadmaps that illustrate the path to career success. However, students often need some of the small, simple maps that they can later compile into the atlases that will define their career journeys.

Of course, we know that some people choose to take adventurous routes in life. Such routes can be challenging and exciting, but they can also be unsettling or even disastrous if the proper precautions are not taken. Some people are more adaptable and resourceful in dealing with unforeseen emergencies along the way. In most cases, however, especially with major trips, people feel more confident when the trip is laid out before them. Students need good "map skills" to maneuver the career paths that lie before them.

A roadmap provides the traveler with the most direct route. Many even choose to call ahead to see if there is any road construction that will require extra time or rerouting. Students who deliberately plan their career paths feel more confident about where they are headed in life. They have investigated the prospects for success and have charted a course that complements their goals, their budgets, and their itineraries. The best planners have even considered alternative routes to their destination.

In this chapter, lesson plans and worksheets are provided to address five different components of Career Exploration and Planning: The Career Planning Process, Using Career Information, Positive Work Attitudes, Career Decisions, and Job-Seeking Skills. The three lessons for each component provide a variety of opportunities for students to understand both the complexity of career planning and the specific skills needed to be successful in the world of work. This final set of lessons will also provide a framework for students to use in integrating some of the other lessons from previous chapters.

STEP BY STEP
Career Exploration and Planning
"Career Planning Process"

OBJECTIVES:

1. Students will be able to sequence the steps of a simple task.

2. Students will be able to sequence a career-related cartoon and explain reasons for the placement.

3. Students will be able to identify activity titles for each cartoon frame.

SUPPLIES:

Sequencing cartoon (reproducible copy provided)

Glue

Scissors

Blank sheet of paper

PORTFOLIO ENTRY: *Career Exploration and Planning,* Competency Skills, *"Career Planning Process"*

STEP BY STEP

Career Exploration and Planning

"Career Planning and Process"

LESSON	NOTES
1. **Introduction:** In small group, ask students to enumerate the steps in making a peanut butter sandwich. Discuss. Share the results with the large group. (The teacher may want to demonstrate the importance of directions by demonstrating the making of the sandwich.)	
2. **Focus:** Why is it important to do each of the steps in order? Explain.	
3. **Activity:** Have students independently cut out each cartoon box and have them organize them in sequential order, gluing them on a blank sheet of paper. Then encourage them to defend the reasons for their placement to a partner. Post cartoons and discuss. What is happening in each frame? What would happen if the sequence was mixed or reversed?	
4. **Closure:** Ask: Can you suggest a word or two to identify the activity in each frame? (Examples: investigating, applying, accepting, working.)	
5. **Follow-up:** Have students ask parents to sequence and label each cartoon frame, discuss with parents, and bring the results to class.	

Sequencing Cartoon

Answer Key to Sequencing Cartoon

PICTURE THIS
Career Exploration and Planning
"Career Planning Process"

OBJECTIVES:

1. Students will be able to define the term "career."

2. Students will be able to identify pictures of career options and create a collage.

3. Students will be able to label career options on the collage.

SUPPLIES:

A variety of magazines

Glue

Poster board

PORTFOLIO ENTRY: *Career Exploration and Planning,* Competency Skills, *"Develop Skills"*

PICTURE THIS

Career Exploration and Planning

"Career Planning Process"

LESSON	NOTES
1. **Introduction:** Ask students to define the term "career." Suggest that they think of synonyms (e.g., job, work, daily activity, occupation, etc.)	
2. **Focus:** Tell them that this activity will focus on what individuals choose for their working lives.	
3. **Activity:** Supply students with magazines, scissors, glue, and poster board. Ask them to create a collage filled with career-options pictures. Display collages and ask students to identify and label the career options.	
4. **Closure:** Ask: What did you learn from this activity? Who do you know in these career options? Which career options do you like? Why? What does this tell you about the world of work?	
5. **Follow-up:** Ask students to talk to their parents about career options. What did they choose? Why did they make those choices?	

GOING "AEP"
Career Exploration and Planning
"Career Planning Process"

OBJECTIVES:

1. Students will be able to define the three stages of the career planning process.

2. Students will be able to apply the planning sequence to life scenarios.

3. Students will be able to create scenarios for each level.

SUPPLIES:

Career process definitions

Going "AEP" Scenarios worksheet

Answer sheet

PORTFOLIO ENTRY: *Career Exploration and Planning,* Competency Skills, *"Career Planning Process"*

GOING "AEP"
Career Exploration and Planning
"Career Planning Process"

LESSON	NOTES
1. **Introduction:** Tell students that choosing a career is a process. Define process as "a series of actions leading to a particular result." Give examples and/or a demonstration (e.g., becoming a truck driver, a secretary, a physician etc.).	
2. **Focus:** Tell students that the three stages of the career process are: awareness, exploration, and planning. Define each with the use of the Going "AEP" worksheet.	
3. **Activity:** Discuss each stage. In pairs, have students label each scenario with a level. Discuss in small groups. In groups of three, have students create new scenarios. Exchange scenarios among triads and ask each group to label the stages. Discuss in large group and correct/negotiate the labeling.	
4. **Closure:** Ask: What career planning stage are you in? In which stage is this lesson? Why is it important for career planning to be a process?	
5. **Follow-up:** Ask students to discuss the career process stages with their parents. Have students explore with their parents whether they had been exposed to these stages.	

GOING "AEP" WORKSHEET

Career process definitions:

AWARENESS: This stage includes self-knowledge and an understanding of the world of work, with the ability to see connections between the two in making career choices.

EXPLORATION: This stage includes the opportunities to investigate careers through information resources and hands-on experience.

PLANNING: This stage includes a sequence of steps that leads to career training and placement.

GOING "AEP" SCENARIOS

Directions: Label each scenario as Awareness (A), Exploration (E), or Planning (P).

1. ____ Cleo's class visited the courthouse on Law Day. Students met judges, clerks, lawyers, and potential jurors. They also saw the law library, the sheriff's department, and the jail. Upon their return, the teacher asked them to brainstorm all the career options they saw that day and enumerate their duties.

2. ____ Bobbi has a class assignment to interview three employees about the job entry requirements of their positions.

3. ____ Jo has selected courses in chemistry and physics to complete the requirements for nursing school.

4. ____ Rick would like to start an independent hot dog stand business. He asks for advice from the American Association of Retired Business Persons free job counseling service.

5. ____ The seventh-grade teacher at the middle school requires a career option collage from each student. When completed, the posters are laminated and passed on to the third-grade students to be used as placemats for lunch on Career Day.

GOING "AEP" SCENARIOS ANSWER SHEET

1. A, E

   Awareness—Students become aware of career options.

   Exploration—Students delve deeper into the specifics of certain careers.

2. E

   Exploration—The student details the specific requirements of three careers.

3. P

   Planning—The student has chosen specific courses to meet entry requirements of a chosen career.

4. E, P

   Exploration—The student investigates the steps necessary to start a business.

   Planning—The student starts to plan and decide if the options are feasible.

5. A

   Awareness—Students look at career options as they appear in the media. Third-grade students are introduced to a variety of careers.

Career Exploration and Planning
"Using Career Information"

OBJECTIVES:

1. Students will be able to define four career categories.

2. Students will be able to brainstorm jobs in the four career categories.

3. Students will be able to pantomime job skills related to each category.

SUPPLIES:

Vocational resource material, such as: *Occupational Outlook Handbook* (1996) Washington, DC: U.S. Department of Labor, Bureau of Labor Statistics.

PORTFOLIO ENTRY: *Career Exploration and Planning,* Competency Skills, *"Develop Skills"*

GET D-I-P-T
Career Exploration and Planning
"Using Career Information"

LESSON	NOTES
1. **Introduction:** Tell students that there are four broad career categories—jobs that deal with: data, ideas, people, things. (Suggest that they remember the categories by using the memory helper, "D-I-P-T.")	
2. **Focus:** Discuss each category in small groups, and have students brainstorm specific jobs in each area.	
3. **Activity:** Individually, have students investigate a job using vocational resources (e.g., *Occupational Outlook Handbook*). After deciding which category the job belongs to, ask volunteers to pantomime the job skills needed for the job, while students guess the category.	
4. **Closure:** Ask: What are the four job categories? How do they differ? Which category appeals to you? Why?	
5. **Follow-up:** Have students explain categories to their parents and categorize their parents' jobs. Survey the class and create a graph.	

OBJECTIVES:

1. Students will be able to identify jobs that students perform in school.

2. Students will be able to identify skills associated with those jobs.

3. Students will be able to identify those skills that will be transferable to adult career choices.

SUPPLIES:

Chart paper

Markers

PORTFOLIO ENTRY: *Career Exploration and Planning*, Competency Skills, *"Work Attitudes"*

BUSY BEES
Career Exploration and Planning
"Using Career Information"

LESSON	NOTES
1. **Introduction:** Tell students that they will be exploring jobs that students perform in school.	
2. **Focus:** In small groups, ask them to brainstorm as many school jobs as possible. (Examples: washing boards, running messages, etc.)	
3. **Activity:** In pairs, have students take five jobs from the brainstormed list and identify the skills required for each job. (Example: Messenger—knowing locations, being accurate, following directions, being responsible.) Then have them brainstorm adult jobs that need the same skill (Example: secretary, page, telephone operator.) Give ample time to complete examples. In large group, ask students to share their examples. Chart responses.	
4. **Closure:** Ask: What conclusions can you draw from this lessons? How do your present job experiences prepare you for the future?	
5. **Follow-up:** Encourage students to broaden their job experiences by volunteering for community service projects.	

FACT FINDING MISSION
Career Exploration and Planning
"Using Career Information"

OBJECTIVES:

1. Students will be able to identify and locate available career resource information at school and in the local community.

2. Students will be able to identify the type of information found in each resource.

3. Students will be able to evaluate the research material and make recommendations about them.

SUPPLIES:

Dictionary of Occupational Titles (1991) Washington, DC: U.S. Department of Labor, Bureau of Labor Statistics.

Occupational Outlook Handbook (1996) Washington, DC: U.S. Department of Labor, Bureau of Labor Statistics.

Computer information

"Fact Finding Mission" Resource List (provided)

PORTFOLIO ENTRY: *Career Exploration and Planning,* Competency Skills, *"Develop Skills"*

FACT FINDING MISSION
Career Exploration and Planning
"Using Career Information"

LESSON	NOTES
1. **Introduction:** Tell students that library resources are available to research a career option. (Students may be assigned a resource.)	
2. **Focus:** Tell students that they will be spending time in the library to identify what resources are available to them.	
3. **Activity:** Pass out worksheet and explain the example. Provide the class with library/computer time to find the resources, with the help of the specialist in each area. (Encourage students to do similar research at their local libraries.) In small groups, have students share their findings.	
4. **Closure:** Ask: Which resource provided the best information? Which did you like the best? Are there enough resources to do a job search?	
5. **Follow-up:** Ask students to make recommendations to the librarian if enough resources were not available to complete the assiqnment.	

FACT FINDING MISSION
RESOURCE LIST

Example:

Resource: *Encyclopedia of Careers & Vocational Guidance*, Vols. 1-3

Edition: _____   Date _____

Location in the library: Reference-left of front desk

Format: vol. 1 review of career fields

            vol. 2 selecting a career

            vol. 3 selecting a technical career

Information available: extensive information on each topic in each volume

----

Resource: _____

Edition: _____   Date _____

Location in the library: _____

Format: _____

Information available: _____

Resource: _____

Edition: _____   Date _____

Location in the library: _____

Format: _____

Information available: _____

Resource: _____

Edition: _____   Date _____

Location in the library: _____

Format: _____

Information available: _____

Resource: _____

Edition: _____   Date _____

Location in the library: _____

Format: _____

Information available: _____

Resource: _____

Edition: _____   Date _____

Location in the library: _____

Format: _____

Information available: _____

Resource: _____

Edition: _____   Date _____

Location in the library: _____

Format: _____

Information available: _____

A CLEARER PICTURE
Career Exploration and Planning
"Positive Work Attitudes"

OBJECTIVES:

1. Students will be able to identify the possible job responsibilities of their parents/guardians.

2. Students will be able to complete an interview with their parents/guardians about their actual job responsibilities.

3. Students will be able to compare the information gathered and draw conclusions from the interviews about the variety and complexities of the world of work.

SUPPLIES:

"A Clearer Picture" Student Worksheet

"A Clearer Picture" Parent Worksheet

PORTFOLIO ENTRY: *Career Exploration and Planning,* Competency Skills, *"Positive Work Attitudes"*

A CLEARER PICTURE
Career Exploration and Planning
"Positive Work Attitudes"

LESSON	NOTES

1. **Introduction:** Tell students that they will be investigating the details of their parents'/guardians' jobs.

2. **Focus:** Ask students to brainstorm on the worksheet the responsibilities they connect with those jobs. In small groups, discuss these responsibilities and have students add to their lists, if appropriate. Collect the sheets.

3. **Activity:** Have students conduct interviews with their parents/guardians or a significant adult regarding their job responsibilities. Allow three days for this project.
   In class, distribute student worksheets and have them compare the information with parent worksheets. Ask: What is similar? different? What new information did you learn?

4. **Closure:** Ask: What did you learn about the world of work? Why is it important to know the details of a job? How can hidden job responsibilities affect your attitude about work? What would be a positive effect? negative?

5. **Follow-up:** Have students reach consensus about the ten most important things to remember about job responsibilities. Post the list for future reference and/or publish it for participating parents. Submit the list to the school newspaper/newsletter.

A CLEARER PICTURE
STUDENT WORKSHEET

Student: _____ Date: _____

Directions: Fill in the blanks.

My parent's/guardian's job is _____

I think the responsibilities of this job might be:

1. _____

   _____

2. _____

   _____

3. _____

   _____

4. _____

   _____

5. _____

   _____

(Return this worksheet to your teacher.)

A CLEARER PICTURE
PARENT/GUARDIAN
INTERVIEW WORKSHEET

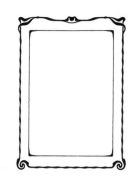

Student: _____ Date: _____

Directions: Interview your parent/guardian and have them discuss their job responsibilities:

Name of job:

Responsibilities:

_____

_____

_____

_____

_____

What is the most important thing to remember about being a good worker?

_____

_____

_____

_____

_____

(Return this worksheet to your teacher.)

RANK ATTITUDE
Career Exploration and Planning
"Positive Work Attitudes"

OBJECTIVES:

1. Students will be able to list the jobs they do at home.

2. Students will be able to rank their attitudes as they perform these jobs.

3. Students will be able to analyze the quality of performance as it relates to the attitude.

SUPPLIES:

"Rank Attitude" Worksheet

PORTFOLIO ENTRY: *Career Exploration and Planning,* Competency Skills, *"Positive Work Attitudes"*

RANK ATTITUDE
Career Exploration and Planning
"Positive Work Attitudes"

LESSON	NOTES
1. **Introduction:** Tell students that they will be doing some analyzing in this lesson. Ask them to mention a number of activities they enjoy doing at home.	
2. **Focus:** In pairs, ask them to brainstorm jobs they are expected to perform at home, and list them on the worksheet. Discuss the scoring. Individually, have students rank all the jobs as they relate to their attitudes.	
3. **Activity:** When that is completed, ask them to go back and rank how well they perform each task without regard to the attitude. Compare the scores, and in large group, discuss how attitude plays a part in performing quality tasks.	
4. **Closure:** Ask: What small steps could be taken to change the attitude about your least favorite job? Are incentives helpful? Why? What kind? Can you create personal incentives?	
5. **Follow-up:** Make a plan to change an attitude. Make a written commitment and check it in two weeks.	

Name _____ **Date** _____

RANK ATTITUDE WORKSHEET

Directions: List ten jobs you are expected to perform at home and rank them as shown:

Ranking: 4—Cool   3—OK   2—So-So   1—Not So Hot

JOBS	ATTITUDE	PERFORMANCE
1.		
2.		
3.		
4.		
5.		
6.		
7.		
8.		
9.		
10.		

RANK ATTITUDE WORKSHEET

Directions: List ten jobs you are expected to perform at home and rank them as shown:

Ranking: 4—Cool   3—OK   2—So-So   1—Not So Hot

JOBS	ATTITUDE	PERFORMANCE
1. get up on time	3	4
2. clean room	1	1
3. do homework	3	3
4. water houseplants	3	4
5. water garden	2	3
6. feed fish	1	3
7. clean fishtank	1	3
8. take out trash	1	2
9. put dirty clothes in clothes hamper	2	2
10. set the table	3	4

MYTH STORY
Career Exploration and Planning
"Positive Work Attitudes"

OBJECTIVES:

1. Students will be able to define the term "myth."

2. Students will be able to brainstorm and investigate myths about work.

3. Students will be able to categorize and draw conclusions about work myths and identify how they affect work attitudes.

SUPPLIES:

Dictionary

Chart paper

PORTFOLIO ENTRY: *Career Exploration and Planning,* Competency Skills, *"Decision Making"*

MYTH STORY
Career Exploration and Planning
"Positive Work Attitudes"

LESSON	NOTES
1. **Introduction:** Tell students that they will be defining and investigating the word "myth," as it relates to the world of work.	
2. **Focus:** Using a dictionary and other resources, have students define and give examples of ancient and modern-day myths.	
3. **Activity:** In small groups, have students brainstorm potential myths about work. (Examples: Pay raises are regular and based on performance; Most holidays are vacation days; You are given prior notice about working overtime.) Ask for volunteers who will ask adults for examples of when work myths affected them. (This should take about three days.) Have students share their stories and information. Have students generate common "themes" from the stories (e.g., fairness, lack of information, budget priorities, etc.) Have students draw conclusions about the information.	
4. **Closure:** Ask: How do your conclusions affect your attitude about future employment? Why is that important to understand? What myths did you hold before this activity?	
5. **Follow-up:** Share conclusions with parents or publish in school newspaper.	

OBJECTIVES:

1. Students will be able to individually list potential career choices and add to that list in a small group.

2. Students will be able to categorize the career choices into clusters: data, people, things, ideas.

3. Students will be able to connect their personal strengths with a career cluster and support the choice.

SUPPLIES:

Chart paper

Markers

LESSON	NOTES

1. **Introduction:** Tell students that they will be attempting a class challenge: to pick a three-digit number (e.g., 150) and to brainstorm that many career choices.

2. **Focus:** Give students 5 minutes to brainstorm individually and then meet in a small group for 15 minutes to make additions to their lists.

3. **Activity:** Review the four career clusters of data, ideas, people, things. (See "Get D-I-P-T" lesson, page 192.) On four pieces of chart paper, have students categorize each career cluster in a different color marker. (Some careers may be in more than one category.)

   Individually, have students list their personal strengths (refer to the Self-Knowledge chapter, Employability Skills section, pages 54–61). Ask students to connect their personal strengths with one career cluster. Ask them to support their viewpoint.

4. **Closure:** Ask: What did you learn from this lesson? Why is it important to know career clusters? Why is it important to know how you connect to the clusters? How difficult was it to brainstorm your strengths? Why? Do you fall into more than one career cluster? Is that a problem?

CRITIC'S CHOICE
Career Exploration and Planning
"Career Decisions"

OBJECTIVES:

1. Students will be able to recognize a career decision-making process.

2. Students will be able to critique the steps in the career decision-making process.

3. Students will be able to make recommendations for the career decision-making process and draw conclusions from the process.

SUPPLIES:

"Critic's Choice" worksheet

Chart paper

Markers

PORTFOLIO ENTRY: *Career Exploration and Planning*, Competency Skills, *"Decision Making"*

CRITIC'S CHOICE
Career Exploration and Planning
"Career Decisions"

LESSON	NOTES
1. **Introduction:** Tell students that they will be given a decision-making process to discuss, critique, and make recommendations upon.	
2. **Focus:** Give students the "Critic's Choice" worksheet. Discuss each step.	
3. **Activity:** In small groups, ask students to critique the process by following the procedure on the worksheet. Discuss in large group and chart the changes. Apply the steps to a hypothetical career choice. Ask students what they might do to apply each step.	
4. **Closure:** Ask: What conclusions can you draw from this lesson? How can you use the process in your daily decision making? How can you use it in career decision making?	

CRITIC'S CHOICE WORKSHEET

CAREER DECISION-MAKING PROCESS:

1. Study yourself.

2. Gather information.

3. Think of alternatives/consequences.

4. Compare and weigh alternatives/consequences.

5. Make a tentative decision-making plan.

6. Create a plan.

7. Evaluate the plan.

CRITIQUE THE PROCESS

Directions: Answer the following questions about the career decision-making process above.

What did I like about it? _____

_____

_____

What should be added? _____

_____

_____

How can I use this now? _____

_____

_____

What else should I consider? _____

_____

_____

CRITIC'S CHOICE WORKSHEET

CAREER DECISION-MAKING PROCESS:

1. Study yourself.
2. Gather information.
3. Think of alternatives/consequences.
4. Compare and weigh alternatives/consequences.
5. Make a tentative decision-making plan.
6. Create a plan.
7. Evaluate the plan.

CRITIQUE THE PROCESS

Directions: Answer the following questions about the career decision-making process above.

What did I like about it? _I learned that making some decisions can be very hard sometimes._ _It means you have to be extra careful. The steps show what you have to think about._

What should be added? _Directions for how to study yourself._ _How do yu know when one alternative is better than another one?_

How can I use this now? _My parents want me to choose something to occupy my_ _time this summer. I need to let them know by next week. This process can help me, I hope._

What else should I consider? _What really matters to me_

PUBLIC DEFENDING
Career Exploration and Planning
"Career Decisions"

OBJECTIVES:

1. Students will be able to identify their one most viable career choice and defend that choice.

2. Students will be able to receive feedback on their choices from three significant adults.

3. Students will be able to record the feedback and discuss it with classmates.

SUPPLIES:

"Public Defending" worksheet

"Public Defending" Reaction worksheet

PORTFOLIO ENTRY: *Career Exploration and Planning,* Results of Career Assessment, *"Pre-Employment Experience"*

PUBLIC DEFENDING
Career Exploration and Planning
"Career Decisions"

LESSON	NOTES
1. **Introduction:** Tell students that they will be applying the decision-making process as it relates to choosing a career.	
2. **Focus:** Ask students to choose one possible career. Tell them they will be defending their choices to three significant individuals for feedback.	
3. **Activity:** Have students list three significant adults with whom they could discuss and defend their career choice. Model an appropriate presentation. (See "Public Defending" worksheet.) Tell students to defend their choices to the three chosen adults and record their comments on the "Public Defending" Reaction worksheet. Discuss the comments in small groups. Have students report their findings to the larger group.	
4. **Closure:** Ask: What new information did you learn from this activity? Do you agree with the opinions of the adults? Why? Why not? How will this activity help you make a more definite career decision?	

PUBLIC DEFENDING WORKSHEET

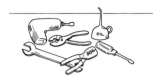

SAMPLE CAREER CHOICE: Teacher

REASONS:
- like school
- like to work with children
- B+ grades
- am creative
- student helper in grades 3 and 4
- mother is a teacher

SAMPLE CAREER CHOICE: Auto Mechanic

REASONS:
like to work with my hands
have helped to rebuild an engine
like to work with tools
will take auto mechanics at
    the vocational center
good problem solver
job security—always broken cars
good salary

NAME: _____

PERSONAL CAREER CHOICE: _____

REASONS:

1. _____

   _____

2. _____

   _____

3. _____

   _____

4. _____

   _____

5. _____

   _____

PUBLIC DEFENDING
REACTION SHEET

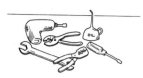

Name: _____   **Career Choice:** _____

POSITIVE OPINIONS	NEGATIVE OPINIONS
Adult:	
Adult:	
Adult:	

SALES PITCH
Career Exploration and Planning
"Job-Seeking Skills"

OBJECTIVES:

1. Students will be able to identify positive work skills in themselves.

2. Students will be able to identify positive work skills in classmates.

3. Students will be able to choose students to work in a cooperative group based on their positive work skills.

SUPPLIES:

None

SALES PITCH
Career Exploration and Planning
"Job-Seeking Skills"

LESSON	NOTES
1. **Introduction:** Tell students that they will be "selling" themselves by investigating their positive work skills.	
2. **Focus:** Have students individually list their positive group project work skills.	
3. **Activity:** Appoint or have students elect cooperative small group leaders. Ask students individually to "sell" themselves as workers to the group leaders, using their brainstormed list. Have leaders choose team members based on their strengths, giving positive reasons for their choices until all students are selected.	
4. **Closure:** Ask: What did you learn from this activity? How will this help you when applying for a job? What parts of this activity were difficult for individual students? What parts were difficult for the leader?	
5. **Follow-up:** In cooperative small project groups, have leaders monitor whether the strengths of each individual are being utilized appropriately.	

OBJECTIVES:

1. Students will be able to identify the occupations of fictitious characters on television.

2. Students will be able to identify the positive and negative work habits of fictitious characters.

3. Students will be able to identify their reasons for their opinions.

SUPPLIES:

Chart paper

PORTFOLIO ENTRY: *Career Exploration and Planning,* Competency Skills, *"Positive Work Attitudes"*

THE POWER OF THE STARS
Career Exploration and Planning
"Job-Seeking Skills"

LESSON	NOTES
1. **Introduction:** Ask students to give examples of fictitious television or movie characters and their jobs (e.g., Batman, the Nanny, Murphy Brown, Homer Simpson).	
2. **Focus:** Ask: Would you hire these characters for their job skills? (A response at this time is not necessary.)	
3. **Activity:** Choose ten of these popular television characters. Based on their positive job skills, list them in priority order. Ask students to be able to support their choices with examples. In small groups, ask students to compare and contrast their choices. Ask each group to choose their top five candidates. Re-group the class into two large groups and have each choose its top three candidates. In the large group, chart the positive qualities that each of the top candidates exhibits.	
4. **Closure:** Ask: Which listed characteristic do you find to be the most positive trait to possess on the job? Which do you think is the most negative? Why? How do you display these positive and negative characteristics now?	

OBJECTIVES:

1. Students will be able to participate in an election.

2. Students will be able to identify the "selling" qualities of each candidate.

3. Students will be able to apply these factors as they relate to job seeking.

SUPPLIES:

Chart paper

Markers

Pictures of three popular cartoon, TV, or movie stars

PORTFOLIO ENTRY: *My Personal Career Plan,* Job-Seeking Skills

YOU'VE GOT MY VOTE
Career Exploration and Planning
"Job-Seeking Skills"

LESSON	NOTES
1. **Introduction:** Tell students that they will be doing some thinking about how people get elected to office.	
2. **Focus:** Hold up the pictures of three popular TV or cartoon characters and ask students to privately vote for their favorite person.	
3. **Activity:** In large group, ask students to brainstorm the qualities of each candidate that "sell" them as a person. Discuss the importance of each quality. Then ask: How are these qualities important to someone when applying for a job? (Examples: neat appearance, sense of humor, ability to work with others, etc.).	
4. **Closure:** Ask: What did you learn from this lesson? How can you develop job "selling qualities" at your age? Is it important to develop those qualities now? Why?	

A Look in the Rearview Mirror

Reflections on Lessons for Life

An educator who practices the art of "reflective learning" looks back on a lesson and examines how things went and how things could be improved. Furthermore, the reflective learner seeks insight from the lessons that will nurture future growth within the profession. The attached evaluation sheets are offered as resources to help in this reflective process. You will need to make multiple copies so that you can evaluate individual lessons and assess student receptivity to both the activities and the objectives. While there is much more to reflection than student and self-evaluation, you are encouraged to use these evaluations as two sets of information that can be used for program reflection and refinement.

As we reflect on the experience of creating these *Lessons for Life,* we are excited about the opportunities that students will have for analyzing, synthesizing, and evaluating the various facets of their career development. As we have talked with educators and shared some of the lessons, we have repeatedly heard the message, "I wish I had had some experiences like these when I was in school!" As a part of our own learning process, we have found personal meaning in many of these lessons because we, too, are lifelong learners who are constantly making meaning of our own career journeys. If life is a journey, we hope we have provided some of the pages of the atlas, as well as some insights about how to enjoy the trip.

FACILITATOR'S EVALUATION SHEET

Lesson Title: _____ Level: _____

Were the objectives met?   Yes   No

Were supplies adequate?   Yes   No

The best part of the lesson/unit: _____

_____

_____

_____

Suggestions to improve the lesson: _____

_____

_____

_____

Comments: _____

_____

_____

_____

Here's what I learned about myself as an instructor/learner: _____

_____

_____

_____

STUDENT EVALUATION SHEET

Lesson Title: _____

This lesson taught me: _____

_____

_____

_____

The best part of this lesson was: _____

_____

_____

_____

Suggestions to improve this lesson are: _____

_____

_____

_____

Here's what I learned about myself: _____

_____

_____

_____

Comments: _____

_____

_____

_____

NOTES

NOTES

NOTES

NOTES

NOTES

NOTES

NOTES

NOTES

NOTES

NOTES

NOTES